To

From

Date

Kingdom Connection

. . . The Orientation To Kingdom Lifestyle

THE CORNERSTONE
PUBLISHING

Joseph Olowe

Kingdom Connection

. . . The Orientation To Kingdom Lifestyle

Paperback ISBN: 978-1-944652-66-1

eBook ISBN: 978-1-944652-67-8

Published by:

Cornerstone Publishing
A Division of Cornerstone Creativity Group LLC
Info@thecornerstonepublishers.com
www.thecornerstonepublishers.com

516.547.4999

Author's Contact

For booking to speak at your next event or to order bulk copies of this book please use information below:

P. O Box 10499
El Paso, TX 79995
1-800-561-9170 or + 1 915-478-8807
www.drjosepholowe.com | info@drjosepholowe.com

DEDICATION

This book is dedicated to a man I have never met but who has influenced my life in the area of prayer and fasting. I refer to him as my friend, Pastor Jentezen Franklin, who encouraged me to be a part of his ministry's 21 days of fasting. This book was born out of that encounter with destiny. Thus, I've decided to title the book after the name of his ministry's TV program. I will forever be grateful for your influence and leadership.

ACKNOWLEDGMENTS

I will like to appreciate my savior Jesus Christ from whom all blessings flow. My sincere gratitude to my wife and partner in ministry, Omolade for her relentless pursuit of excellence for our family first and ministry.

To my children Olamide, Simi and Dare who have given me an opportunity to practice what I am preaching.

To my ministry team, first to my able editor who I consider as a gift from heaven to me, Pastor Joseph Ola and to Daniel Emonido who I refer to as mighty Danny, for all the divine graphics; many thanks. To Pastor Gbenga Showunmi and his professional team at Cornerstone Publishing, thank you for making this dream come true.

To a good friend of mine, Pastor David Olayemi — the first man apart from my family, who sincerely believed in my writing gift and encouraged me to pursue my dream — may the God of heaven never forget your labor of love.

CONTENTS

Part Four: Go to God for Everything

INTRODUCTION

JESUS IS OUR KING

In today's world, we are consumed with many statistics about events around us. For example, we read that we have a birthrate of 62.5 per hundred women between the ages fifteen and forty-four, an infant mortality rate of 6.07 deaths per 1,000 live births, an overall mortality rate of 807.3 per 100,000 people, and a life expectancy of 78.7 years in the United States (CDC). According to the United States Census Bureau, more than sixteen percent of the population is living in poverty. These are alarming statistics. What is more alarming, however, is the statistics of the church of Christ. Nineteen percent of the body of Christ does a hundred percent of the giving. No wonder the church is always playing catch-up.

An even bigger problem we face in the church today is the apparent inability to provide an atmosphere for new believers coming into our churches to actually stay after they have accepted Jesus Christ as their personal Lord and Savior.

The Bible tells us this problem did not begin with our generation. It has been happening since the days when Jesus walked the earth. How can we remedy this problem? Answering that question is the sole purpose of writing this book.

It appears that Christianity is the only "organization" that falls short in the area of providing orientation for a new member. In the secular organizations, when a new employee is hired, he or she spends a considerable amount of time in orientation but this seems to be lacking or inadequate in many churches. After looking at this apparent inadequacy in many churches, I sat down and tried to come up with a way to provide a new believer, a not-so-new believer, and even an established believer a "shot of faith" so they can truly live the kingdom lifestyle.

He said,

> *"Therefore, A certain nobleman went into a far country to receive for himself a kingdom, and to return. And he called his ten servants, and delivered them ten pounds, and said unto them, 'Occupy till I come.' But his citizens hated him, and sent a message after him, saying, 'We will not have this man to reign over us.' And it came to pass, that when he was returned, having received the kingdom, then he commanded these servants to be called unto him, to whom he had given the money, that he might know how much every man had gained by trading. Then came the first, saying, 'Lord, thy pound hath gained ten pounds.' And he said unto him, 'Well, thou good servant: because thou hast been faithful in a very little, have thou authority over ten cities.' And the second came, saying, 'Lord, thy pound hath gained five pounds.' And he said likewise to him, 'Be thou also over five cities.' And another came, saying,*

> *'Lord, behold, here is thy pound, which I have kept laid up in a napkin: For I feared thee, because thou art an austere man: thou takest up that thou layedst not down, and reapest that thou didst not sow.' And he saith unto him, 'Out of thine own mouth will I judge thee, thou wicked servant. Thou knewest that I was an austere man, taking up that I laid not down, and reaping that I did not sow: Wherefore then gavest not thou my money into the bank, that at my coming I might have required mine own with usury?' And he said unto them that stood by, 'Take from him the pound, and give it to him that hath ten pounds.' (And they said unto him, 'Lord, he hath ten pounds.') For I say unto you, 'That unto every one which hath shall be given; and from him that hath not, even that he hath shall be taken away from him. But those mine enemies, which would not that I should reign over them, bring hither, and slay them before me.'" (Luke 19:12-27 emphasis added)*

In this parable told by Jesus, we read about ten servants. One of the servants gained ten pounds, one had a gain of five pounds, and the third person did not gain anything. Most messages I've heard preached from this passage of scripture rebuke the third guy because he did not do anything with what he was given by the nobleman, soon-to-be king. However, my focus this time is not on the one who did not produce, but on the seven who seem to have gotten lost in the process. Where did these other seven "servants" go?

The passage says, "But his citizens hated him, and sent a message after him, saying, 'We will not have this man to reign over us.' It seemed that an outright rebellion occurred among the other seven because as soon as the nobleman left to be crowned as king, my best guess is that these seven "servants" left their positions serving the soon-to-be king and went back to their previous lives and activities.

When I read what happened to those other seven servants, my heart ached. The king said of them, "But those mine enemies, which would not that I should reign over them, bring hither, and slay them before me."

These former servants were suddenly declared enemies by the king.

The church of God is growing, but if out of every ten believers, one is extremely productive, one is better than average, one is not productive but stays in service to Jesus, the King of kings, then seven are completely lost back to the world, then such statistics reflect extreme failure. When we see the King of kings face to face, what will be our excuse?

A twenty percent success rate for the church is an "F" grade even by the world's standards. If a company were to experience such a turnover in their employee base, they would seriously reevaluate their training and orientation plan. So the purpose of this book is to introduce a concept whereby the church organization can have an orientation package for every new and seasoned believer so that we can raise our success rate and truly begin impacting our world. Every believer needs to understand and learn to live the kingdom lifestyle.

For any new convert to enjoy the full benefits of the new birth, he or she has to break his or her "alabaster box" so that people are able to smell the new aroma of the new found faith. Until the box is broken, new converts appear no different than they were before their salvation experience. There is no evidence of the new life if all they are doing is carrying around their new found faith in an alabaster box. It is difficult for the people around new believers to know the value of what they are carrying around until they break out of the old and allow the new life to spread into every area of their lives. Speaking of the alabaster box, in Mark 14:3-9, we see that even Judas realized the value of what was in the woman's alabaster box.

> *And being in Bethany in the house of Simon the leper, as he sat at meat, there came a woman having an alabaster box of ointment of spikenard very precious; and she brake the box, and poured it on his head. And there were some that had indignation within themselves, and said, Why was this waste of the ointment made? For it might have been sold for more than three hundred pence, and have been given to the poor. And they murmured against her. And Jesus said, Let her alone; why trouble ye her? She hath wrought a good work on me. For ye have the poor with you always, and whensoever ye will ye may do them good: but me ye have not always. She hath done what she could: she is come aforehand to anoint my body to the burying. Verily I say unto you, Wheresoever this gospel shall be preached throughout the whole world, this also that she hath done shall be spoken of for a memorial of her.*

When you come to Jesus after you receive Him as your Lord and Savior, you receive an alabaster box that contains a fragrance that needs to be broken so that people around you can begin to savor it. Many people will be upset at you and tell you that you are wasting your time in service to the King, but Jesus is saying that what you are doing is vital to His kingdom advancement. He wants people to hear what God is doing in and through you. It will bring glory to God and will serve as a testimony that might bring even more people to the knowledge of Christ and what He did for them.

Another reason we must provide an orientation package for new believers is to instruct them that the devil is lurking around, and he's not happy about their decision to follow Jesus Christ. It is vitally important that they come to understand how to deal with this very real enemy. Here is an example of this with Job, who was considered a righteous man.

> *Now there was a day when the sons of God came to present themselves before the Lord, and Satan came also among them. And the Lord said unto Satan, Whence comest thou? Then Satan answered the Lord, and said, From going to and fro in the earth, and from walking up and down in it. And the Lord said unto Satan, Hast thou considered my servant Job, that there is none like him in the earth, a perfect and an upright man, one that feareth God, and escheweth evil? (Job 1:6-8)*

When you were without Christ, the devil knew that you belonged to his camp so he did little to disturb you. Once you have made a decision for God, you come up on his radar. It is very important for every Christian to be shielded from demonic interference and this is done through a healthy feeding of the Word of God. What you feed on is of utmost importance. The world is ready to feed you its "facts" if you are willing to eat it. The Bible gives us an example of this important principle from the life of Daniel and his three friends.

> *And the king spake unto Ashpenaz the master of his eunuchs, that he should bring certain of the children of Israel, and of*

the king's seed, and of the princes; Children in whom was no blemish, but well favoured, and skillful in all wisdom, and cunning in knowledge, and understanding science, and such as had ability in them to stand in the king's palace, and whom they might teach the learning and the tongue of the Chaldeans. And the king appointed them a daily provision of the king's meat, and of the wine which he drank: so nourishing them three years, that at the end thereof they might stand before the king. Now among these were of the children of Judah, Daniel, Hananiah, Mishael, and Azariah: Unto whom the prince of the eunuchs gave names: for he gave unto Daniel the name of Belteshazzar; and to Hananiah, of Shadrach; and to Mishael, of Meshach; and to Azariah, of Abed–nego. But Daniel purposed in his heart that he would not defile himself with the portion of the king's meat, nor with the wine which he drank: therefore he requested of the prince of the eunuchs that he might not defile himself. Now God had brought Daniel into favour and tender love with the prince of the eunuchs. And the prince of the eunuchs said unto Daniel, I fear my lord the king, who hath appointed your meat and your drink: for why should he see your faces worse liking than the children which are of your sort? Then shall ye make me endanger my head to the king. Then said Daniel to Melzar, whom the prince of the eunuchs had set over Daniel, Hananiah, Mishael, and Azariah, Prove thy servants, I beseech thee, ten days; and let them give us pulse to eat, and water to drink. Then let our countenances be looked upon before thee, and the countenance of the children that eat of the portion of the king's meat: and as thou seest, deal with thy servants. So he consented to them in this matter, and proved them ten days. And at the end of ten days their countenances appeared fairer and fatter in flesh than all the children which did eat the portion of the king's meat. Thus Melzar took away the portion of their meat, and the wine that they should drink;

and gave them pulse. (Daniel 1:3-16 emphasis added)

The king wanted these boys fed with certain types of food so that their "look" would conform to that of his kingdom, but Daniel knew that God's ways were far superior to that of the king and determined in his heart not to defile himself. In the same vein, the god of this age, Satan, is ready to feed the believer the meal of his domain so as to conform us to his domain's lifestyle. As believers we need to watch what we feed our spirit with, otherwise our spiritual growth will be stunted. As a believer matures in the things of God and develops his or her relationship with Him, it is important to continually focus on the principles of the kingdom and live according to its lifestyle. Without a King and a knowledge of the King's principles, people do what is right in their own sight.

In those days there was no king in Israel, but every man did that which was right in his own eyes. (Judges 17:6 emphasis added)

In those days there was no king in Israel: and in those days the tribe of the Danites sought them an inheritance to dwell in; for unto that day all their inheritance had not fallen unto them among the tribes of Israel. (Judges18:1 emphasis added)

And it came to pass in those days, when there was no king in Israel, that there was a certain Levite sojourning on the side of mount Ephraim, who took to him a concubine out of Bethlehem Judah. (Judges 19:1 emphasis added)

In those days there was no king in Israel: every man did that which was right in his own eyes. (Judges 21:25)

It is a biblical principle that in the mouth of two or three witnesses, truth is established. Four times, as stated above, the importance of having a king was laid bare. Simply put, the absence of a king brings lack of direction. It makes people wander and do whatever they want. Once we have chosen to follow the King of kings, Jesus Christ, it is very important that we are shown how to live the kingdom lifestyle.

For the purpose of this orientation, we shall look at the word KING as an acronym and study what each letter stands for and how we can get the maximum benefit out of our relationship with Jesus, our King. It is through the knowledge of God, the Father, and Jesus Christ, the Son, that grace and peace is multiplied in our lives and the lives we are called to influence.

> *Grace and peace be multiplied unto you through the knowledge of God, and of Jesus our Lord. (2 Peter 1:2)*

Jesus is our King, so we need to:

K—Know Him.

I—Invest Time in Study, Prayer, Fasting, Giving, and Praise.

N—Nothing Shall Separate Us from Him.

G—Go to Him for Everything.

It is time to get to know our King and receive all the benefits of living the kingdom lifestyle.

PART ONE

K - KNOW HIM

That I may know him, and the power of his resurrection, and the fellowship of his sufferings, being made conformable unto his death. (Philippians 3:10 emphasis added).

The main question most believers ask is how do we know Him? I believe that if you are reading this book, you have made a commitment to follow Jesus, by accepting Him as your personal Lord and Savior. Peradventure you are reading this book and you have not yet made that decision, today is your day of salvation. The first step is to know about God's great love for you and what He did to make a way for you to become a resident of His Kingdom—forever.

For God so loved the world, that he gave his only begotten Son, that whosoever believeth in him should not perish, but have everlasting life. For God sent not his Son into the world to condemn the world; but that the world through him might be saved. He that believeth on him is not condemned: but he that believeth not is condemned already, because he hath not believed in the name of the only begotten Son of God. (John 3:16-18)

While we were yet sinners, Christ was given for us because God loved this world so much that He did not want us to remain in our disconnected state. It is very important to know that there is no amount of good we can do to earn God's love. It is impossible for us to save ourselves.

For all have sinned, and come short of the glory of God; being justified freely by his grace through the redemption that is in Christ Jesus. (Romans 3:23-24)

We have all sinned, but we are justified freely by His grace through the redemption that is in Christ Jesus.

That if thou shalt confess with thy mouth the Lord Jesus, and shalt believe in thine heart that God hath raised him from the dead, thou shalt be saved. For with the heart man believeth unto righteousness; and with the mouth confession is made unto salvation. For the scripture saith, Whosoever believeth on him shall not be ashamed. For there is no difference between the Jew and the Greek: for the same Lord over all is rich unto all that call upon him. For whosoever shall call upon the name of the Lord shall be saved. (Romans 10:9-13 emphasis added)

It is free, but we have to make a personal declaration of our faith individually and surrender totally to Him. You can do this right away by saying this simple prayer:

Lord Jesus, I come to you and surrender my will to You. I accept You as my personal Lord and Savior. From now on I know I am a child of God. Thank You, God, for Your great love for me.

Congratulations, you have just been numbered in heaven as a redeemed of the Lord. Now that you are born again, your mind needs to be renewed so that you can live a life that conforms to your confession. It is time to learn how to put off the old and put on the new so you can live the kingdom lifestyle.

Therefore if any man be in Christ, he is a new creature: old things are passed away; behold, all things are become new. (2 Corinthians 5:17)

CHAPTER 1

PUT ON THE NEW MAN

And such as do wickedly against the covenant shall he corrupt by flatteries: but the people that do know their God shall be strong, and do exploits. (Daniel 11:32 emphasis added)

Now that you know God, you are going to be strong enough to do great exploits in His name. You are now a representative and an ambassador of the King of kings. You are called to do exploits which are striking—notable deeds, feats of strength, and spirited or heroic acts.

One of the first questions new believers often ask has to do with how they can know the will of God for their lives. We are not the first to ask this question—it is a question dealt with in the Bible.

I beseech you therefore, brethren, by the mercies of God, that ye present your bodies a living sacrifice, holy, acceptable unto God, which is your reasonable service. And be not conformed to this world: but be ye transformed by the renewing of your

> *mind, that ye may prove what is that good, and acceptable, and perfect, will of God. (Romans 12:1-2 emphasis added)*

The Bible affirms this possibility because at the time of our new birth, we become something brand new. This metamorphosis begins on the inside of us and gradually transforms every part of our life. Many of the things we used to say and do now feel wrong to us. Our inner desires have changed which will gradually change our outer actions as we learn to present our bodies as a living sacrifice to God. However, God gives us choices just like He did Adam and Eve in the Garden of Eden.

We have to choose to put on this new man and allow the new us to emerge and become the driving force of our lives.

This new creature—this new identity of being in Christ as a child of God—you will develop as you realize you were created in the image of the King and are part of His royal family. The old, previous moral lifestyle is no longer appropriate. A new life has begun.

> *And have put on the new man, which is renewed in knowledge after the image of him that created him. (Colossians 3:10 emphasis added)*

A simple analogy will help you understand this principle. When you work for a specific business or organization, you are often required to wear a uniform that identifies you with them. You can often tell what a person does for a living by the kind of clothes they are wearing. When you see a mechanic, you know immediately what he does because his clothes are covered with grease stains. However, if that same mechanic is invited to come and see the president or the king of the nation, he will quickly go home to change and put on his best clothes to honor the president or king.

You and I are being invited to come and see the King of kings, as a child of the King. Therefore, it is highly important to do away with our old clothes of morality and put on our new royal robes by renewing our mind with the Word of God. To put on Jesus as a new creation, we have to get rid of our present "clothing" or mindset.

Christians also have a dress code as part of the army of the King. That's why this book is a package that contains information needed to thrive in the kingdom. We are His children, but we are also called to function as productive members in His kingdom. In order to do this, we have to put on the whole armor of God.

> *Finally, my brethren, be strong in the Lord, and in the power of his might. Put on the whole armor of God, that ye may be able to stand against the wiles of the devil. For we wrestle not against flesh and blood, but against principalities, against powers, against the rulers of the darkness of this world, against spiritual wickedness in high places. Wherefore take unto you the whole armor of God, that ye may be able to withstand in the evil day, and having done all, to stand. Stand therefore, having your loins girt about with truth, and having on the breastplate of righteousness; And your feet shod with the preparation of the gospel of peace; Above all, taking the shield of faith, wherewith ye shall be able to quench all the fiery darts of the wicked. And take the helmet of salvation, and the sword of the Spirit, which is the word of God: Praying always with all prayer and supplication in the Spirit, and watching thereunto with all perseverance and supplication for all saints. (Ephesians 6:10-18)*

Kingdom Connection

It is important to our kingdom lifestyle that we understand the purpose of each piece of this important armor.

- The belt of truth is Jesus because John 14:6 says Jesus is the Truth.
- The breastplate of righteousness has its link in the Son of righteousness (Malachi 4:2; 1 Corinthians 1:30).
- The boots we are to wear are the boots of peace. Jesus is the Prince of Peace (Isaiah 9:6).
- Our shield of faith links up with Jesus who is the Author and Finisher of our faith (Hebrews 12:2).
- Our helmet is salvation and Jesus is the Savior (Matthew 1:21).
- Our sword is the Word of God and the Lord Jesus is the Word made flesh (John 1:14).

Notice that all the components of our armor are linked to Jesus. No wonder we are commanded to put on Jesus. Romans 13:14 says, "But put ye on the Lord Jesus Christ, and make not provision for the flesh, to fulfil the lusts thereof." After we have received Him as our Lord and Savior and renewed our minds, we put on the Lord Jesus Christ and wear Him everywhere we go.

JESUS IS THE WAY, THE TRUTH, AND THE LIFE

Not only is Jesus the truth and the giver of this new life, He is the only way to God. In today's world there are so many who claim to have the path that leads to God, but

Jesus clearly said He is the only one way to eternal life.

> *Jesus saith unto him, I am the way, the truth, and the life: no man cometh unto the Father, but by me. If ye had known me, ye should have known my Father also: and from henceforth ye know him, and have seen him. (John 14:6-7 emphasis added)*

> *I am the door: by me if any man enter in, he shall be saved, and shall go in and out, and find pasture. The thief cometh not, but for to steal, and to kill, and to destroy: I am come that they might have life, and that they might have it more abundantly. I am the good shepherd: the good shepherd giveth his life for the sheep. (John 10:9-11 emphasis added)*

There is a thief who will try to get you off the right path, but Psalm 23 says when you follow a good shepherd you shall not want, you will lie down in green pastures; he will lead you beside the still water, restore your soul and lead you in the right path; you will fear no evil, you will be comforted, your cup will run over, and goodness and mercy will follow you all the days of your life. You can only get these through Jesus who cares about His people. Jesus not only said He is the way and truth, He said He is the bread of life.

> *I am that bread of life. This is the bread which cometh down from heaven, that a man may eat thereof, and not die. I am the living bread which came down from heaven: if any man eat of this bread, he shall live forever: and the bread that I will give is my flesh, which I will give for the life of the world. The Jews therefore strove among themselves, saying, How can this man give us his flesh to eat? Then Jesus said unto them, Verily, verily, I say unto you, Except ye eat the flesh of the Son of man, and drink his blood, ye have no life in you. Whoso eateth*

> *my flesh, and drinketh my blood, hath eternal life; and I will raise him up at the last day. For my flesh is meat indeed, and my blood is drink indeed. He that eateth my flesh, and drinketh my blood, dwelleth in me, and I in him. (John 6:48, 50-56)*

This brings us to another important part of our relationship with Him. We are called to communion with Him. He talks about eating His flesh and drinking His blood, but Jesus was not suggesting that we become cannibalistic. He is telling us about having communion with Him in a very intimate way. It is just like when we get to know someone and they invite us to their house to dine with them. The same is true of our Lord and Savior, Jesus. Our time with Him gives us the power to maintain the kingdom lifestyle on a daily basis. Communion introduces us to the new covenant and reminds us of the benefit of that covenant especially as we enter this new lifestyle.

> *And he took bread, and gave thanks, and brake it, and gave unto them, saying, This is my body which is given for you: this do in remembrance of me. Likewise also the cup after supper, saying, This cup is the new testament in my blood, which is shed for you. (Lukeu22:19-20)*

> *For I have received of the Lord that which also I delivered unto you, That the Lord Jesus the same night in which he was betrayed took bread: And when he had given thanks, he brake it, and said, Take, eat: this is my body, which is broken for you: this do in remembrance of me. After the same manner also he took the cup, when he had supped, saying, This cup is the new testament in my blood: this do ye, as oft as ye drink it, in remembrance of me. For as often as ye eat this bread, and drink this cup, ye do shew the Lord's death till he come. (1 Corinthians 11:23-26)*

JESUS IS OUR RIGHTEOUSNESS

> *For he hath made him to be sin for us, who knew no sin; that we might be made the righteousness of God in him. (2 Corinthians 5:21 emphasis added)*

> *But to him that worketh not, but believeth on him that justifieth the ungodly, his faith is counted for righteousness. Even as David also describeth the blessedness of the man, unto whom God imputeth righteousness without works, Saying, Blessed are they whose iniquities are forgiven, and whose sins are covered. Blessed is the man to whom the Lord will not impute sin. (Romans 4:5-8)*

So what is righteousness? To be righteous is to act in accordance with divine or moral law; be free from guilt or sin; and be morally right or justifiable. The Vine's Dictionary says, "It was formerly spelled 'rightwiseness,' which clearly expresses the meaning. It is the gracious gift of God to men whereby all who believe on the Lord Jesus Christ are brought into right relationship with God. This righteousness is unattainable by obedience to any law, or by any merit of man's ability, or any other condition than that of faith in Christ.".

> *Knowing that a man is not justified by the works of the law, but by the faith of Jesus Christ, even we have believed in Jesus Christ, that we might be justified by the faith of Christ, and not by the works of the law: for by the works of the law shall no flesh be justified. (Galatians 2:16)*

Jesus gives us right standing with God—it is not what we do, or our good deeds—it is Jesus's finished work that gives us right standing.

Therefore, we need to quit trying to please God by our own works. We need to enjoy the grace that was made available to us by the cross, because no flesh can make it without Jesus. It is all about God's grace. God's grace is available through His Son, Jesus Christ.

The grace of God is the engine that drives the life of a successful Christian. Grace is the oxygen that the Christian needs to breathe. Grace is "the love and mercy given to us by God, not because of anything we have done to earn it; the condescension or benevolence shown by God toward the human race. It is a spontaneous gift from God to man, generous, free, totally unexpected, and undeserved that takes the form of divine favor, love, and clemency" (Wikipedia).

The first time grace is mentioned in the Bible is in Genesis which resulted in the salvation of Noah's family and the living creatures on earth during the devastating flood. God then established His covenant with Noah. When God gives grace, it is always associated with His covenant with us.

> *But Noah found grace in the eyes of the Lord. (Genesis 6:8 emphasis added)*

God's mercy and grace was on Joseph in Genesis 39:4, when He made him an overseer of Potiphar's house. God's mercy and grace was on Esther as she became the queen in Esther 2:17. Even Jesus needed grace while on earth, *"And the child grew and became strong in spirit, filled with wisdom; and the grace of God was upon Him" (Luke 2:40).* We need God's mercy and grace to have dominion over sin and we are justified by His grace.

Romans 6:14 says, "For sin shall not have dominion over you: for you are not under the law, but under grace" (emphasis added).

Romans 3:24 says, "Being justified freely by His grace through the redemption that is in Christ Jesus" (emphasis added).

Romans 4:16 tells us, "Therefore it is of faith that it might be according to GRACE, so that the promise might be sure to all seed, not only to those who are of the law, but also to those who are of the faith of Abraham, who is the father of us all. We are qualified for the promise according to grace" (emphasis added).

Romans 5:1-2 explains, "Therefore being justified by faith, we have peace with God through our Lord Jesus Christ: By whom also we have access by faith into this grace in which we stand, and rejoice in hope of the glory of God" (emphasis added).

We need the mercy and grace of God to continue our journey before we see Him face to face. Grace is available at all times to help us live the kingdom lifestyle. The Apostle Paul talks about grace in his letters to the Corinthians to instruct them in the kingdom lifestyle. Corinth was a wealthy trading center and also a very wicked city, so it was difficult for the Christians there not to act like their neighbors.

But by the grace of God I am what I am: and his grace which was bestowed upon me was not in vain; but I laboured more abundantly than they all: yet not I, but the grace of God which was with me. (1 Corinthians 15:10 emphasis added)

We then, as workers together with him, beseech you also that ye receive not the grace of God in vain. (2 Corinthians 6:1 emphasis added)

And God is able to make all grace abound toward you; that ye, always having all sufficiency in all things, may abound to every good work. (2 Corinthians 9:8 emphasis added)

"All grace" simply refers to every favor and earthly blessing that will come to us in abundance through living the kingdom lifestyle. Lack disappears in a life full of grace. We can ask God for help in times of need because He has made adequate provision for us through Jesus.

However, it is possible to frustrate His grace by trying to have right standing with Him through works instead of through Jesus, the only way to righteousness.

Let us therefore come boldly unto the throne of grace, that we may obtain mercy, and find grace to help in time of need. (Hebrews 4:16 emphasis added)

And he said unto me, My grace is sufficient for thee: for my strength is made perfect in weakness. Most gladly therefore will I rather glory in my infirmities, that the power of Christ may rest upon me. (2 Corinthians 12:9 emphasis added)

I do not frustrate the grace of God: for if righteousness come by the law, then Christ is dead in vain. (Galatians 2:21 emphasis added)

God's grace can do amazing things in a believer's life. Grace can be our speech therapist, prevent the root of bitterness from taking hold within us, and help us to remain humble before Him. We need to strive to grow in grace and the knowledge of Jesus Christ, our Lord and Savior.

Let your speech be always with grace, seasoned with salt, that ye may know how ye ought to answer every man. (Colossians 4:6 emphasis added)

Looking diligently lest any man fail of the grace of God; lest any root of bitterness springing up trouble you, and thereby many be defiled. (Hebrews 12:15 emphasis added) But he giveth more grace. Wherefore he saith, God resisteth the proud, but giveth grace unto the humble. (James 4:6 emphasis added)

But grow in grace, and in the knowledge of our Lord and Saviour Jesus Christ. To him be glory both now and forever. (2 Peter 3:18 emphasis added)

The last verse of the Bible is about grace.

"The grace of our Lord Jesus Christ be with you all. Amen" (Revelation 22:21).

CHAPTER 2

THE MANY NAMES OF GOD

And they that know thy name will put their trust in thee: for thou, Lord, hast not forsaken them that seek thee. (Psalm 9:10)

Why is it important that we know and understand the many names of God as we begin to imbibe the kingdom culture? Each of God's names has a significant meaning as we develop a sound relationship with Him. For us to develop a close relationship with an individual, we have to know them by name. The same is true with our King. The verse above states that they that know His name will put their trust in Him, which simply means as we develop our relationship with Him, our level of trust increases.

Because he hath set his love upon me, therefore will I deliver him: I will set him on high, because he hath known my name.

> *He shall call upon me, and I will answer him: I will be with him in trouble; I will deliver him, and honor him. (Psalm 91:14-15)*

The names of God describe His attributes, so as we study the names of God, it will take us into another dimension of our knowledge of Him. We cannot even call somebody our friend if we don't know his or her "name" and what that "name" stands for. For example, the name, Judas, is synonymous with betrayal. Proverbs 22:1 tells us a "good name" is more desirable than great riches. When you know someone's name and know what that name stands for, the level of relationship is taken to another level. It is the same with God. We will begin by looking at what God told Moses about His name.

> *And I appeared unto Abraham, unto Isaac, and unto Jacob, by the name of God Almighty, but by my name Jehovah was I not known to them. (Exodus 6:3).*

If we compare the names of Jehovah to a government cabinet system, it may be easier to understand why knowing His names and what they mean is so important to our kingdom lifestyle. For example, in the U.S. government, there is the Secretary of State, the Secretary of Defense, and the Secretary of Agriculture to name a few. If you want to get a U.S. passport you will not go to the Secretary of Agriculture, you would ask for the Secretary of State. Let us look at some of the names of Jehovah, so we know what "name" to call upon depending on our prevalent circumstances.

- Jehovah Nissi - The Lord My Banner (Exodus 15:17)
- Jehovah-Raah - The Lord My Shepherd (Psalm 23:1,

80:1; Genesis 48:15, 49:24)

- Jehovah Rapha - The Lord That Heals (Exodus 15:26, Isaiah 30:26, 61:1; Jeremiah 30:17, 3:22; Psalm 103:3)
- Jehovah Shammah - The Lord Is There (Ezekiel 48:35)
- Jehovah Tsidkenu - The Lord Our Righteousness (Jeremiah 23:6, 33:16)
- Jehovah Makaddesh - The Lord Who Sanctifies You (Exodus 31:13; Leviticus 20:8)
- Jehovah El Olam - The Lord the Everlasting God (Genesis 21:33; Jeremiah 10:10; Isaiah 26:4)
- Jehovah Elohim – The Lord our Creator (Genesis 1:1)
- Jehovah Qanna - Jealous (Exodus 20:5, 34:14; Deuteronomy 4:24, 5:9, 6:15)
- Jehovah Jireh - The Lord Will Provide (Genesis 22:14)
- Jehovah Shalom - The Lord Is Peace (Judges 6:24)
- Jehovah Sabaoth - The Lord of Hosts (1 Samuel 1:3, 11, 17:45; 2 Samuel 6:18, 7:27; 1 Kings 19:14; 2 Kings 3:14; 1 Chronicles 11:9; Psalm 24:10, 48:8, 80:4, 19, 84:3 (Courtesy of the Blue Letter Bible)

In the Lord's Prayer, Jesus said when we pray we are to say, "Hallowed be Thy name." That means we are to honor and respect His name. To hallow a thing is to make it holy, sanctify, and consecrate it. The third commandment says we are not to misuse or take the name of God in vain, that is we are not to take it lightly or frivolously in false affirmations or profanely (Exodus 20:7).

Kingdom Connection

The Lord hear thee in the day of trouble; the name of the God of Jacob defend thee. (Psalm 20:1)

The name of the God of Jacob will defend us in our times of trouble. I don't think we can fully comprehend the power in this Bible verse until we look into the meaning of "defend." Defend means to ward off attack; guard against assault or injury; maintain by argument, evidence; contest a legal charge or claim; serve as an attorney; support in the face of criticism; and prove the validity of something by answering arguments and questions put by a committee of specialists.

The name of the Lord is a strong tower: the righteous runneth into it, and is safe. (Proverbs 18:10)

Our help is in the name of the Lord, who made heaven and earth. (Psalm 124:8)

God is our refuge and strength, a very present help in trouble. Therefore will not we fear, though the earth be removed, and though the mountains be carried into the midst of the sea; Though the waters thereof roar and be troubled, though the mountains shake with the swelling thereof. (Psalm 46:1-3)

I am the Lord: that is my name: and my glory will I not give to another, neither my praise to graven images. (Isaiah 42:8)

God does not share His glory with anyone or anything.

Some of us want to take credit when God uses us as a point of blessing for someone. Beware, you might be cutting yourself short of a future opportunity to be a co-worker with Him by trying to take His glory. If you attribute our successes to our smartness, education, wealth, looks, and status in the community, beware—that is taking His glory as well. He does not share His glory or praise with any graven image no matter what shape or form it might take.

> *Therefore my people shall know my name: therefore they shall know in that day that I am he that doth speak: behold, it is I. (Isaiah 52:6)*

> *Even every one that is called by my name: for I have created him for my glory, I have formed him; yea, I have made him. (Isaiah 43:7)*

EMMANUEL – GOD WITH US

Who is Jehovah? He is Emmanuel, God with us. "Behold, a virgin shall be with child, and shall bring forth a son, and they shall call his name Emmanuel, which being interpreted is, God with us" (Matthew 1:23 emphasis added).

> *For unto us a child is born, unto us a son is given: and the government shall be upon his shoulder: and his name shall be called Wonderful, Counsellor, The mighty God, The everlasting Father, The Prince of Peace. Of the increase of his government and peace there shall be no end, upon the throne of David, and upon his kingdom, to order it, and to establish it with judgment and with justice from henceforth even forever. The zeal of the Lord of hosts will perform this. (Isaiah 9:6-7 emphasis added)*

Wonderful means excellent, great, and marvelous. When you know Him as a wonder-working God, He will always perform wonders for you as Jehovah El Elyon

Counsellor is a person who counsels, a lawyer. We will never go wrong if we know Him as a counsellor, Jehovah Adonai.

The mighty God means having unlimited power; omnipotent. No wonder the Bible says for with God nothing shall be impossible—Jehovah Elohim; our El Shaddai.

The everlasting Father means He's a Father that lasts forever or continues for an indefinitely long time. The Bible says He make all things beautiful in His time, He does not keep time like we do. When we relate with Him at this level, patience will have its perfect work in us; Jehovah El Olam.

Prince of Peace. *"Thou wilt keep him in perfect peace, whose mind is stayed on thee: because he trusteth in thee" (Isaiah 26:3)*, Jehovah Shalom.

What a great privilege we have to receive Jesus, God Who dwells in His worshippers.

> *Wherefore God also hath highly exalted him, and given him a name which is above every name: That at the name of Jesus every knee should bow, of things in heaven, and things in earth, and things under the earth; And that every tongue should confess that Jesus Christ is Lord, to the glory of God the Father. (Philippians 2:9-11)*

Let us look into other things the name of the Lord can do for us or what it is we can gain from the wonderful name of Jesus.

> *My little children, these things write I unto you, that ye sin not. And if any man sin, we have an advocate with the Father, Jesus Christ the righteous. (1 John 2:1).*

Every one of us has been created by God for His glory. So whatever you are going through now is part of the plan to showcase you for His glory. Each of us has been called for a purpose.

> *And we know that all things work together for good to them that love God, to them who are the called according to his purpose. (Romans 8:28).*

Jesus said, *"My sheep hear my voice, and I know them, and they follow me" (John 10:27)*, but *"a stranger will they not follow, but will flee from him: for they know not the voice of strangers" (John 10:5)*. If you don't know His name, you may not recognize His voice and you may follow a stranger instead of the Lord. To truly live the kingdom lifestyle, you must be able to follow His voice and go where He leads.

THE REVELATION OF JESUS CHRIST

> *The Revelation of Jesus Christ, which God gave unto him, to shew his servants things that must shortly come to pass; and he sent and signified it by his angel unto his servant John: Who bear record of the word of God, and the testimony of Jesus Christ, and of all things that he saw. Blessed is he that readeth, and they that hear the words of this prophecy, and keep those things which are written therein: for the time is at hand. (Revelation 1:1-3)*

> *And I saw heaven opened, and behold a white horse; and he that sat upon him was called Faithful and True, and in righteousness he doth judge and make war. His eyes were as a flame of fire, and on his head were many crowns; and he had a name written, that no man knew, but he himself. And he was clothed with a vesture dipped in blood: and his name is called The Word of God. (Revelation 19:11-13)*

> *And he hath on his vesture and on his thigh a name written, King of kings, and Lord of lords. (Revelation 19:16)*

> *Behold, I come quickly: hold that fast which thou hast, that no man take thy crown. Him that overcometh will I make a pillar in the temple of my God, and he shall go no more out: and I will write upon him the name of my God, and the name of the city of my God, which is new Jerusalem, which cometh down out of heaven from my God: and I will write upon him my new name. (Revelation 3:11-12)*

It is very important that we know His name so that we can recognize His voice. In today's world there are different "winds of doctrine," which we must watch out for. We do not want to be like little children who are carried about by every "wind of doctrine" that comes our way. There are many out there that will try to deceive us and tempt us to move off the path to kingdom living.

> *That we henceforth be no more children, tossed to and fro, and carried about with every wind of doctrine, by the sleight of men, and cunning craftiness, whereby they lie in wait to deceive. (Ephesians 4:14)*

OUR COVENANT-KEEPING GOD

A covenant means a strong commitment and loyalty. Every covenant contains promises and terms that are specific to it. There are actually two kinds of covenant in scripture. One is between man and man and the other is between God and man. The Bible records eight covenants between God and man. God is a God of covenant and each covenant reveals His perfect will and purpose for man (Psalm 111), and reflects His love, grace, and mercy. He relates with us by His covenant. Let us look at what He does with covenant.

> *Know therefore that the Lord thy God, he is God, the faithful God, which keepeth covenant and mercy with them that love him and keep his commandments to a thousand generations. (Deuteronomy 7:9)*

Many businesses today offer rewards for doing business with them. For example, in the airline industry you earn miles each time you fly. When you get a new job, one of the most important things you consider before accepting the job is the benefits package. There are restaurants now that will basically give you food for free if you are a loyal customer. The same is true with God. When we agree to the terms of His covenant with us, we receive the promises listed in that covenant. The only way to know and understand His benefits package is to study His Word.

> *Bless the Lord, O my soul: and all that is within me, bless his holy name. Bless the Lord, O my soul, and forget not all his benefits: Who forgiveth all thine iniquities; who healeth all thy diseases; Who redeemeth thy life from destruction; who crowneth thee with lovingkindness and tender mercies; Who satisfieth thy mouth with good things; so that thy youth is renewed like the eagle's. (Psalm 103:1-5)*

FORGET NOT ALL HIS BENEFITS

What are the benefits of knowing the Lord?

- He forgives all our iniquities: Life insurance because He forgives our sins—past, present and future—and guarantees us eternal life.

- He heals our diseases: Health insurance; remember you don't have to meet any deductible or co-pay because it was all paid for on the cross (Exodus 23:25-26).
- He redeems our lives from destruction: Round the clock security (Psalm 91:4-6).
- He crowns us: I believe this crown symbolizes affluence and wealth. It means you will be paid well.
- He offers rest and renewal: Big vacation package, "And he said unto them, Come ye yourselves apart into a desert place, and rest a while: for there were many coming and going, and they had no leisure so much as to eat. And they departed into a desert place by ship privately" (Mark 6:31-32).

> *There remaineth therefore a rest to the people of God. For he that is entered into his rest, he also hath ceased from his own works, as God did from his. Let us labour therefore to enter into that rest, lest any man fall after the same example of unbelief. (Hebrews 4:9-11)*

GOOD THINGS TO COME

> *But Christ being come an high priest of good things to come, by a greater and more perfect tabernacle, not made with hands, that is to say, not of this building. (Hebrews 9:11)*

What good thing is to come? According to the original translation, it is the benefit and blessing of Jesus because He paid for it all on the cross.

> *I know that, whatsoever God doeth, it shall be forever: nothing can be put to it, nor any thing taken from it: and God doeth it, that men should fear before him. (Ecclesiastes 3:14)*

God has the final authority and He has given us all that pertains to life and godliness. Please make sure you enjoy your benefits for being a member of His kingdom to the fullest.

> *Grace and peace be multiplied unto you through the knowledge of God and or Savior Jesus Christ, according to his divine power hath given unto us all things that pertain unto life and godliness, through the knowledge of him that hath called us to glory and virtue: whereby are given unto us exceeding great and precious promises: that by these ye might be partakers of the divine nature, having escaped the corruption that is in the world through lust. (2 Peter 1:2-4)*

KEY POINTS FROM PART ONE

- A big problem is our inability to get new believers to actually stay planted after they accept Jesus Christ as their personal Lord and Savior.
- These former servants were suddenly declared enemies by the king.
- Every believer needs to understand and learn to live the kingdom lifestyle.
- We have to choose to put on this new man and allow the new us to emerge and become the driving force of our lives.
- Jesus gives us right standing with God, so it is not what we do, or our good deeds, it is Jesus's finished work that gives us right standing.
- It is possible to frustrate His grace by trying to have

right standing with Him through works instead of through Jesus, the only way to righteousness.

- God does not share His glory with anyone or anything.

PART TWO

I - INVEST IN THE KINGDOM OF GOD

We are now on the second part of our journey to understanding the kingdom lifestyle. Here, we will learn what it means to invest in the kingdom of God. Invest means to put (money) to use, by purchase or expenditure, in something offering potential profitable returns, as interest, income, or appreciation in value. Invest is to use, give, or devote (time, talent, etc.) as for a purpose or to achieve something. It also means to furnish with power, authority, right or rank; to endow with a quality or, characteristic.

There are many areas of our lives that we can invest our time, talent, and money into like buying a house or a car, setting money aside for college for our children, putting money in stocks and bonds, or even starting a business. We invest in these areas to prepare a better future for ourselves and our families. When we come into the family of God, the same things holds true.

We need to invest our time in the study of the Word of God, prayer, service, fasting, and in praise and worship. We need to invest our money to further the cause of the kingdom. Remember: somebody, somewhere, invested in the church or fellowship wherever you gave your life to Jesus. It is your turn to do it for someone else so they will hear the gospel and make a decision for Jesus. What a way to use our time, talents, and money.

Give, and it shall be given unto you; good measure, pressed down, and shaken together, and running over, shall men give into your bosom. For with the same measure ye mete withal it shall be measured to you again. (Luke 6:38)

CHAPTER 3

INVEST IN THE WORD

And of the children of Issachar, which were men that had understanding of the times, to know what Israel ought to do; the heads of them were two hundred; and all their brethren were at their commandment. (1 Chronicles 12:32)

Having the understanding of the times we live in is very important to our development in the kingdom of God. We know that there are many things competing for our attention. It is highly imperative to know what the Word of God is saying to us at all times, so that we can remain alert and focused.

Studying the Word will put us in command of the world we live in.

We need to remember we are in the world, but we are not of the world (John 15:19). The sons of Issachar were put in charge of the people of Israel because they knew what ought to be done at any given time. For us to have the understanding of the times we live in, we need to invest quality time studying God's Word.

> *Get wisdom, get understanding: forget it not; neither decline from the words of my mouth. Forsake her not, and she shall preserve thee: love her, and she shall keep thee. Wisdom is the principal thing; therefore get wisdom: and with all thy getting get understanding. (Proverbs 4:5-7 emphasis added)*

The Bible says wisdom is the principal thing, we need to get it. Get is a verb, therefore, it is an action word that means to go after or take hold of something. We are told to get understanding. Wisdom equals knowledge plus understanding. That is why we need to have both in order to attain wisdom for kingdom living. Let's look at few Bible verses on the importance of studying the Word of God and being able to understand it.

> *Wherewithal shall a young man cleanse his way? By taking heed thereto according to thy word. (Psalm 119:9)*

> *Thy word have I hid in mine heart, that I might not sin against thee. (Psalm 119:11)*

> *Thy word is a lamp unto my feet, and a light unto my path. (Psalm 119:105)*

> *But whoso looketh into the perfect law of liberty, and continueth therein, he being not a forgetful hearer, but a doer of the work, this man shall be blessed in his deed. (James 1:25)*

> *This book of the law shall not depart out of thy mouth; but thou shalt meditate therein day and night, that thou mayest observe to do according to all that is written therein: for then thou shalt make thy way prosperous, and then thou shalt have good success. (Joshua 1:8)*

But he said, Yea rather, blessed are they that hear the word of God, and keep it. (Luke 11:28)

Search the scriptures; for in them ye think ye have eternal life: and they are they which testify of me. (John 5:39)

But he answered and said, It is written, Man shall not live by bread alone, but by every word that proceedeth out of the mouth of God. (Matthew 4:4)

As newborn babes, desire the sincere milk of the word, that ye may grow thereby. (1 Peter 2:2)

Study to shew thyself approved unto God, a workman that needeth not to be ashamed, rightly dividing the word of truth. (2 Timothy 2:15)

If we need direction or need to make a decision, we should to look into the Word of God. It is the perfect law of liberty. The word testifies of God's power, goodness, and contains all fullness of God's head, but we have to search it. The word that proceeded from the mouth of God is recorded for us in the Bible. Young Christians and not-so-young Christians all need to study the Word of God to grow in wisdom through understanding. To share the gospel with others, we need to study it. Then we can rightly divide it for easy consumption of our listeners.

Some Christians believe their pastors more than the Word of God or feel they cannot study the Word of God for themselves.

And if thou say in thine heart, How shall we know the word which the Lord hath not spoken? When a prophet speaketh in the name of the Lord, if the thing follow not, nor come to pass, that is the thing which the Lord hath not spoken, but the prophet hath spoken it presumptuously: thou shalt not be afraid of him. (Deuteronomy 18:21, 22).

To spend time studying the Word cannot be over emphasized. Here is the summary of the reasons we should do this according to the wisest man who ever lived, Solomon,

To know wisdom and instruction; to perceive the words of understanding; To receive the instruction of wisdom, justice, and judgment, and equity; To give subtlety to the simple, to the young man knowledge and discretion. A wise man will hear, and will increase learning; and a man of understanding shall attain unto wise counsels. (Proverbs 1:2-5)

INVEST IN PRAYER

After this manner therefore pray ye: Our Father which art in heaven, Hallowed be thy name. Thy kingdom come. Thy will be done in earth, as it is in heaven. Give us this day our daily bread. And forgive us our debts, as we forgive our debtors. And lead us not into temptation, but deliver us from evil: For thine is the kingdom, and the power, and the glory, forever. (Matthew 6:9-13)

Prayer is simply talking to God, taking time to pour out our hearts to Him, and God talking back to us. Prayer is a two-way communication. In Genesis 18:20-33, God appeared to Abraham, started a conversation with him, and Abraham communicated back about the situation in Sodom.

And the Lord said, Because the cry of Sodom and Gomorrah is great, and because their sin is very grievous; I will go down

now, and see whether they have done altogether according to the cry of it, which is come unto me; and if not, I will know. And the men turned their faces from thence, and went toward Sodom: but Abraham stood yet before the Lord. And Abraham drew near, and said, Wilt thou also destroy the righteous with the wicked? Peradventure there be fifty righteous within the city: wilt thou also destroy and not spare the place for the fifty righteous that are therein? That be far from thee to do after this manner, to slay the righteous with the wicked: and that the righteous should be as the wicked, that be far from thee: Shall not the Judge of all the earth do right? And the Lord said, If I find in Sodom fifty righteous within the city, then I will spare all the place for their sakes. And Abraham answered and said, Behold now, I have taken upon me to speak unto the Lord, which am but dust and ashes: Peradventure there shall lack five of the fifty righteous: wilt thou destroy all the city for lack of five? And he said, If I find there forty and five, I will not destroy it. And he spake unto him yet again, and said, Peradventure there shall be forty found there. And he said, I will not do it for forty's sake. And he said unto him, Oh let not the Lord be angry, and I will speak: Peradventure there shall thirty be found there. And he said, I will not do it, if I find thirty there. And he said, Behold now, I have taken upon me to speak unto the Lord: Peradventure there shall be twenty found there. And he said, I will not destroy it for twenty's sake. And he said, Oh let not the Lord be angry, and I will speak yet but this once: Peradventure ten shall be found there. And he said, I will not destroy it for ten's sake. And the Lord went his way, as soon as he had left communing with Abraham: and Abraham returned unto his place. (Genesis 18:20-33)

The above conversation was initiated by God Almighty.

Kingdom Connection

In the case of Jabez, a man born into sorrow, he prayed and initiated the conversation with God and the Lord answered,

> *And Jabez was more honorable than his brethren: and his mother called his name Jabez, saying, Because I bare him with sorrow. And Jabez called on the God of Israel, saying, Oh that thou wouldest bless me indeed, and enlarge my coast, and that thine hand might be with me, and that thou wouldest keep me from evil, that it may not grieve me! And God granted him that which he requested. (1 Chronicles 4:9, 10)*

How Do We Pray?

The only way to pray according to God's will is to pray what He has already said in His Word.

We cannot go wrong using God's words in our prayers and conversations with Him.

What do we ask God in prayer?

1. Pray for other people's well-being like Abraham prayed for Sodom and Gomorrah.

2. Jabez prayed for his needs, you can pray for yours as well.

3. Pray for the peace of Jerusalem; in other words, you can pray for your country and leaders (politically and spiritually).

4. Pray for your spouse, your children, and your extended family.

How often do we pray? You can pray as often as you want. Jesus and many other great men and women of faith found it was good to pray in the morning so they could set the tone of their day.

> *And in the morning, rising up a great while before day, he (Jesus) went out, and departed into a solitary place, and there prayed. (Mark 1:35)*

> *And Abraham gat up early in the morning to the place where he stood before the Lord. (Genesis 19:27)*

> *My voice shalt thou hear in the morning, O Lord; in the morning will I (David) direct my prayer unto thee, and will look up. (Psalm 5:3)*

> *With my soul have I desired thee in the night; yea, with my spirit within me will I (Isaiah) seek thee early: for when thy judgments are in the earth, the inhabitants of the world will learn righteousness. (Isaiah 26:9)*

Who helps us with our prayer? The Holy Spirit will help you in prayer when you ask Him to help. If you have not already done so, pray and ask to receive the Holy Spirit with the evidence of speaking in tongues.

> *Likewise the Spirit also helpeth our infirmities: for we know not what we should pray for as we ought: but the Spirit itself maketh intercession for us with groanings which cannot be uttered. And he that searcheth the hearts knoweth what is the mind of the Spirit, because he maketh intercession for the saints according to the will of God. (Romans 8:26, 27)*

Does God answer prayer? From the story of Jabez, we know God granted his request. God will answer yours today, too. Even if your life has been filled with misfortune, prayer can change things for you like it did for Hannah. The Lord that granted Hannah's request will grant yours today as well.

Kingdom Connection

Now Hannah, she spake in her heart; only her lips moved, but her voice was not heard: therefore Eli thought she had been drunken. And Eli said unto her, How long wilt thou be drunken? put away thy wine from thee. And Hannah answered and said, No, my lord, I am a woman of a sorrowful spirit: I have drunk neither wine nor strong drink, but have poured out my soul before the Lord. (1 Samuel 1:13-15)

Simplify Your Prayers

I've learned that simple, heartfelt, full-of-faith prayers always get God's attention.

Unfortunately, we often overlook this and turn our prayers into a big show. We have to beware of talking to impress ourselves or to impress God when we're praying. Sometimes I think we just want to sound eloquent. We want to impress God with our phrases and sound holy. However, God just wants to have a little chat with us. He wants us to talk to Him like we would a friend, not with a different tone of voice. If we don't speak Elizabethan English during the day, we don't need to use it when we pray.

We also don't have to pray for hours on end. It's good to schedule prayer time, but we should just pray until we're finished, and then go about our business until the next time we feel the need to pray some more.

The only way prayer will ever be satisfying is if we simply use it as an opportunity to get God's help and involve Him in everything we do. He's not waiting to be impressed. He wants to live life with you. Don't perform. Just invite Him in.

Prayer Starter: Holy Spirit, don't let me turn prayer into a performance! I don't want to overdo it and try and pray too long just to impress You. I want to invite You, as my closest friend, into every aspect of my life. (Adapted from Joyce Meyers Daily Devotion)

> *And he spake this parable unto certain which trusted in themselves that they were righteous, and despised others: Two men went up into the temple to pray; the one a Pharisee, and the other a publican. The Pharisee stood and prayed thus with himself, God, I thank thee, that I am not as other men are, extortionists, unjust, adulterers, or even as this publican. I fast twice in the week, I give tithes of all that I possess. And the publican, standing afar off, would not lift up so much as his eyes unto heaven, but smote upon his breast, saying, God be merciful to me a sinner. I tell you, this man went down to his house justified rather than the other: for every one that exalteth himself shall be abased; and he that humbleth himself shall be exalted. (Luke 18:9-14)*

CHAPTER 4

INVEST IN PRAISE AND WORSHIP

Praise is thanking God for what He has done, what He is doing, and what He is going to do. Worship is acknowledging God for who He is and beholding His glory in His presence.

Praise and worship are powerful tools that always bring the presence of God into any situation.

> *But thou art holy, O thou that inhabitest the praises of Israel. (Psalm 22:3)*

The word inhabit stood out when I was looking at this Bible verse. It simply means to live or dwell in, to exist or be situated within. That means when you praise God, He literally comes down to live or dwell in that atmosphere. So, if you really want to feel or see His presence praise Him no matter what is going on in your life.

> *Enter into his gates with thanksgiving, and into his courts with praise: be thankful unto him, and bless his name. (Psalm 100:4)*

In other words, anytime I open my mouth to talk to God, I always start my conversation with praise and not complaints or requests.

> *Praise the Lord; for the Lord is good: sing praises unto his name; for it is pleasant. (Psalm 135:3)*

> *Praise ye the Lord. Praise God in his sanctuary: praise him in the firmament of his power. Praise him for his mighty acts: praise him according to his excellent greatness. Praise him with the sound of the trumpet: praise him with the psaltery and harp. Praise him with the timbrel and dance: praise him with stringed instruments and organs. Praise him upon the loud cymbals: praise him upon the high sounding cymbals. Let everything that hath breath praise the Lord. Praise ye the Lord. (Psalm 150:1-6)*

We can praise God for keeping us alive, for the free oxygen we breathe, for provision, for protection, and for providence. As long as we have breath, we must praise the Lord. That is the main reason we were created.

JEHOSHAPHAT

In this story, three tribes came against the king and his kingdom. His subjects came and told him that a great multitude had come to take over his kingdom. At first, he did what any normal human being would do—he panicked; but thereafter, he set himself to seek the Lord. From verses 5 to 13 we know that he prayed to God according to what he read in the Bible regarding God's promises to His people (reaffirming the importance of knowing what the Bible says regarding any situation). Let's look at God's instruction to the king.

Then upon Jahaziel the son of Zechariah, the son of Benaiah, the son of Jeiel, the son of Mattaniah, a Levite of the sons of Asaph, came the Spirit of the Lord in the midst of the congregation; And he said, Hearken ye, all Judah, and ye inhabitants of Jerusalem, and thou king Jehoshaphat, Thus saith the Lord unto you, Be not afraid nor dismayed by reason of this great multitude; for the battle is not yours, but God's. (2 Chronicles 20:14-15)

The Lord told Jehoshaphat that the battle belongs to Him. Then God told the king exactly what to do.

Tomorrow go ye down against them: behold, they come up by the cliff of Ziz; and ye shall find them at the end of the brook, before the wilderness of Jeruel. Ye shall not need to fight in this battle: set yourselves, stand ye still, and see the salvation of the Lord with you, O Judah and Jerusalem: fear not, nor be dismayed; tomorrow go out against them: for the Lord will be with you. (2 Chronicles 20:16-17 emphasis added)

And when he had consulted with the people, he appointed singers unto the Lord, and that should praise the beauty of holiness, as they went out before the army, and to say, Praise the Lord; for his mercy endureth forever. And when they began to sing and to praise, the Lord set ambushes against the children of Ammon, Moab, and mount Seir, which were come against Judah; and they were smitten. (2 Chronicles 20:21, 22)

Jehoshaphat believed God and did what no seasoned warrior would ever do. He stood still and did nothing, and he appointed singers to go out before the army to praise the Lord. Let's see the result of praise and worship against even such a formidable enemy.

And when Judah came toward the watch tower in the wilderness, they looked unto the multitude, and, behold, they were dead bodies fallen to the earth, and none escaped. And when Jehoshaphat and his people came to take away the spoil of them, they found among them in abundance both riches with the dead bodies, and precious jewels, which they stripped off for themselves, more than they could carry away: and they were three days in gathering of the spoil, it was so much. (2 Chronicles 20:24, 25)

Powerful Praise Brings Powerful Results.

Don't let the devil weigh you down. When Satan comes around, just lift your hand and praise the Lord. Purposeful praise brings down the mighty hand of Jehovah to intervene in any situation.

There is another story about Jehoshaphat that teaches us how to engage life's battles without lifting a finger. This story is about King Jehoshaphat of Judah, the king of Edom, and the king of Israel coming together to fight the Moabites.

And he went and sent to Jehoshaphat the king of Judah, saying, The king of Moab hath rebelled against me: wilt thou go with me against Moab to battle? And he said, I will go up: I am as thou art, my people as thy people, and my horses as thy horses. (2 Kings 3:7)

The kings of Judah, Edom, and Israel set out on a seven-day journey to fight the Moabites, but there was a little problem: they lacked water. Let's look at what King Jehoshaphat did in response to the problem.

So the king of Israel went, and the king of Judah, and the

> *king of Edom: and they fetched a compass of seven days' journey: and there was no water for the host, and for the cattle that followed them. And the king of Israel said, Alas! that the Lord hath called these three kings together, to deliver them into the hand of Moab! (2 Kings 3:9-10)*

> *But Jehoshaphat said, Is there not here a prophet of the Lord, that we may enquire of the Lord by him? And one of the king of Israel's servants answered and said, Here is Elisha the son of Shaphat, which poured water on the hands of Elijah. And Jehoshaphat said, The word of the Lord is with him. So the king of Israel and Jehoshaphat and the king of Edom went down to him. (2 Kings 3:11-12)*

Whenever we are in the midst of any problem, we should run towards God not toward someone or something else. Get the Bible and look for the solution right in the Word of God. Look at what Elisha did to get directions from God to make the impossible possible. Here is where we see the power of praise and worship in action.

> *But now bring me a minstrel. And it came to pass, when the minstrel played, that the hand of the Lord came upon him. (2 Kings 3:15)*

The three kings were looking for water to drink and keep their cattle from dying, but Elisha asked for a minstrel. A minstrel was a Medieval singer or musician, i.e. one who sang or recited poetry. Elisha asked for a musician to play an instrument to provide an atmosphere of worship. God inhabits the praises of His people.

> *And he said, Thus saith the Lord, Make this valley full of ditches. For thus saith the Lord, Ye shall not see wind, neither shall ye see rain; yet that valley shall be filled with water, that*

> *ye may drink, both ye, and your cattle, and your beasts. And this is but a light thing in the sight of the Lord: he will deliver the Moabites also into your hand. (2 Kings 3:16-18)*

Because of high praise, they got water and deliverance from their enemies. When you learn to praise God, He will begin to move in the areas that you never think you need help. The rest is history. When the Moabites saw the miracle water, there was an illusion that made the water looked like blood. The arm of flesh will surely fail, but when we engage in purposeful praise and worship we will see purposeful results.

Let Everything That Has Breath Praise The Lord.

> *And they rose up early in the morning, and the sun shone upon the water, and the Moabites saw the water on the other side as red as blood: And they said, This is blood: the kings are surely slain, and they have smitten one another: now therefore, Moab, to the spoil. And when they came to the camp of Israel, the Israelites rose up and smote the Moabites, so that they fled before them: but they went forward smiting the Moabites, even in their country. (2 Kings 3:22-24)*

PAUL AND SILAS

Another example of what praise can do is in the New Testament. It is the story of Paul and Silas in prison. From Acts 15:40, we saw that Paul selected Silas to go with him on the missionary journey confirming the churches in Syria and Cilicia. In Acts 16, we saw how the work of the Lord was progressing. Paul chose Timothy to oversee the work there and then the Holy Spirit led them away from going into Asia and led them to Macedonia instead.

Now when they had gone throughout Phrygia and the region of Galatia, and were forbidden of the Holy Ghost to preach the word in Asia, after they were come to Mysia, they assayed to go into Bithynia: but the Spirit suffered them not. (Acts 16:6-7)

And a vision appeared to Paul in the night; There stood a man of Macedonia, and prayed him, saying, Come over into Macedonia, and help us. And after he had seen the vision, immediately we endeavored to go into Macedonia, assuredly gathering that the Lord had called us for to preach the gospel unto them. (Acts 16:9-10)

We can conclude from the above reading that Paul and Silas were in the perfect will of God for their lives and ministries. Everything was going well for them until verses 16-18.

And it came to pass, as we went to prayer, a certain damsel possessed with a spirit of divination met us, which brought her masters much gain by soothsaying: The same followed Paul and us, and cried, saying, These men are the servants of the most high God, which shew unto us the way of salvation. And this did she many days. But Paul, being grieved, turned and said to the spirit, I command thee in the name of Jesus Christ to come out of her. And he came out the same hour. (Acts 16:16-18)

Sometimes, even when we follow God's directive, certain problems might come our way, but rest assured that He will see us through.

And when her masters saw that the hope of their gains was gone, they caught Paul and Silas, and drew them into the marketplace unto the rulers, and brought them to the magistrates, saying, These men, being Jews, do exceedingly trouble our city. (Acts 16:19-20)

Allegations were leveled against Paul and Silas, which were completely false in Act 16:21-22.

And when they had laid many stripes upon them, they cast them into prison, charging the jailor to keep them safely. (Acts 16:23)

Instead of feeling sorry for themselves and thinking that if they were truly in the will of God things like this should not be happening, Paul and Silas did the exact opposite.

And at midnight Paul and Silas prayed, and sang praises unto God: and the prisoners heard them. (Acts 16:25)

I bolded the word "midnight" for a reason. You might be at the crossroad in your life right now. It might be dark and you feel you have no way out of your particular situation. As you choose to praise and worship God like Paul and Silas did, you will cross over into a new beginning. Read what happened as a result of their praise.

And suddenly there was a great earthquake, so that the foundations of the prison were shaken: and immediately all the doors were opened, and every one's bands were loosed. (Acts 16:26)

From now on there will be a "Suddenly" in your vocabulary.

There will be a great quake that will shake your situation back into the divine order God has ordained for you as you praise the Lord. I have tried it and it works. Just set your alarm to the midnight hour which is 12:00 a.m.

regardless where you are in the world. If Paul and Silas did it at the midnight hour and that was their results, you can do it, too. Every closed door will open immediately for you and every chain will be broken off of you in Jesus' name.

> *Shall the prey be taken from the mighty, or the lawful captive delivered? But thus saith the Lord, Even the captives of the mighty shall be taken away, and the prey of the terrible shall be delivered: for I will contend with him that contendeth with thee, and I will save thy children. And I will feed them that oppress thee with their own flesh; and they shall be drunken with their own blood, as with sweet wine: and all flesh shall know that I the Lord am thy Saviour and thy Redeemer, the mighty One of Jacob. (Isaiah 49:24-26)*

> *And when it was day, the magistrates sent the sergeants, saying, Let those men go. (Acts 16:35)*

Salvation took place in that prison that night. As you release your high praise to God, everything holding you down will let go in Jesus' name. God loves praise and worship so much that He has twenty-four elders worshiping Him 24/7.

When you praise God, there is always a commotion in the kingdom of darkness, and it always results into great victories and wholeness in your situation.

CHAPTER 5

INVEST IN FELLOWSHIP AND SERVICE

Fellowship is the gathering of believers on a platform—be it in a church building or otherwise—whereby they worship God together. Fellowshipping or belonging to a church as a member of the body of Christ is very vital to a believer's growth so that such may not get lost back into the world.

> *I was glad when they said unto me, Let us go into the house of the Lord. (Psalm 122:1)*

What a great benefit we have when we belong to a church as a member. If a person dates and sleeps around with many partners, we say they are promiscuous. Another example might be if a person comes into a house and moves from one seat to another; everyone around will start wondering what is wrong. Our piece of advice to these people is to stay put and make something of their life. The same applies to someone who goes around from one church to another looking for a perfect church. We need to be set in a church so that we can function and become a fulfilled Christian.

> *Not forsaking the assembling of ourselves together, as the manner of some is; but exhorting one another: and so much the more, as ye see the day approaching. (Hebrews 10:25)*

> *And he closed the book, and he gave it again to the minister, and sat down. And the eyes of all them that were in the synagogue were fastened on him. (Luke 4:20)*

> *And when he was departed thence, he went into their synagogue. (Matthew 12:9)*

> *And he taught in their synagogues, being glorified of all. (Luke 4:15)*

> *And he preached in the synagogues of Galilee. (Luke 4:44)*

> *These things said he in the synagogue, as he taught in Capernaum. (John 6:59)*

Jesus visited and taught in many synagogues during His earthly ministry. He said the temple was to be called a house of prayer.

> *And when he had made a scourge of small cords, he drove them all out of the temple, and the sheep, and the oxen; and poured out the changers' money, and overthrew the tables. (John 2:15)*

> *And he went into the temple, and began to cast out them that sold therein, and them that bought; Saying unto them, It is written, My house is the house of prayer: but ye have made it a den of thieves. And he taught daily in the temple. But the chief priests and the scribes and the chief of the people sought to destroy him. (Luke 19:45-47)*

Apostle Paul taught in the synagogues and explained the

main reason we are to belong to a church. We all have different functions and gifts that we are to learn to use within the body of Christ. You are brought into the kingdom for such a time as this; your gifts and talents are needed in your local church. It is more pleasing to God if you allow Him to set you in a local church where you can bring more glory to His name. I have been a member of my home church for about twenty years.

> *And straightway he preached Christ in the synagogues, that he is the Son of God. (Acts 9:20)*

> *And he reasoned in the synagogue every Sabbath, and persuaded the Jews and the Greeks. (Acts 18:4)*

> *For as we have many members in one body, and all members have not the same office. (Romans 12:4)*

> *For as the body is one, and hath many members, and all the members of that one body, being many, are one body: so also is Christ. (1 Corinthians 12:12)*

> *But now hath God set the members every one of them in the body, as it hath pleased him. (1 Corinthians 12:18).*

INVEST IN SERVICE

Service is simply an act of help; being at the disposal of another for a good cause. Using your time to serve at your local church cannot be overemphasized. Being a member is a great thing, and being a participating member takes it to another level. The Lord Jesus asks us to always have a servant's heart. How do we develop a servant's heart? David had a great heart for service to God and gives us many great examples.

For a day in thy courts is better than a thousand. I had rather be a doorkeeper in the house of my God, than to dwell in the tents of wickedness. (Psalm 84:10)

A person with a servant's heart desires to serve others.

Another sign of a committed Christian is their commitment to God's work. In most churches, this is referred to as volunteering in different areas of ministry. I encourage you to get involved. The Bible encourages us to be fervent in the spirit and in serving the Lord. What is your commitment to God and your local church? Do you go to be served by others? Are you a bench warmer? Do you go to serve the Lord in any way that you can?

Not slothful in business; fervent in spirit; serving the Lord. (Romans 12:11)

Another thing that God expects from us when we serve is not to be slothful. God wants us to have the spirit of excellence while we work for Him. There are different ministries at different churches. For example, the church I attend has a bus ministry, bookstore, cafe, care ministry, clothing ministry, food pantry, greeters, guest services, information center, jail and prison ministry, kids ministry, a video department, nursery ministry, parking and security, performing arts ministries, dance ministry, drama ministry, small group ministry, ushers and youth ministry. For about eight years I have served as a greeter, and enjoy welcoming people to the service.

But he that is greatest among you shall be your servant. (Matthew 23:11)

And whosoever will be chief among you, let him be your servant. (Matthew 20:27)

Blessed is that servant, whom his lord when he cometh shall find so doing. (Matthew 24:46)

Let this mind be in you, which was also in Christ Jesus: Who, being in the form of God, thought it not robbery to be equal with God: But made himself of no reputation, and took upon him the form of a servant, and was made in the likeness of men: And being found in fashion as a man, he humbled himself, and became obedient unto death, even the death of the cross. (Philippians 2:5-8)

People with servant's heart are generally generous, humble, and become more faithful in their dealings with God.

Being a servant is not limited to God's work. It also makes you want to serve your spouse, children, neighbor, and your country. When we do, our lives becomes more valuable to God and we become an asset to His kingdom. This is a vital part of the kingdom lifestyle.

And the servant of the Lord must not strive; but be gentle unto all men, apt to teach, patient. (2 Timothy 2:24)

For we are labourers together with God: ye are God's husbandry, ye are God's building. (1 Corinthians 3:9).

INVEST OUR MONEY

We are called to invest our time, talents, and money in the work of the body of Christ.

Solomon, the wisest man that ever lived, said money is

very important for us to advance the kingdom. Everything that happens in the house of God requires money.

> *A feast is made for laughter, and wine maketh merry: but money answereth all things. (Ecclesiastes 10:19)*

> *Then answered I them, and said unto them, The God of heaven, he will prosper us; therefore we his servants will arise and build: but ye have no portion, nor right, nor memorial, in Jerusalem. (Nehemiah 2:20)*

> *And thou say in thine heart, My power and the might of mine hand hath gotten me this wealth. But thou shalt remember the Lord thy God: for it is he that giveth thee power to get wealth, that he may establish his covenant which he sware unto thy fathers, as it is this day. (Deuteronomy 8:17, 18)*

The only reason money or wealth comes to is for us to build His kingdom and establish His covenant. Just like any other business, churches must have money to meet its obligations. The Bible has given us specific instructions on how we are to bring money into the kingdom.

> *Then there shall be a place which the Lord your God shall choose to cause his name to dwell there; thither shall ye bring all that I command you; your burnt offerings, and your sacrifices, your tithes, and the heave offering of your hand, and all your choice vows which ye vow unto the Lord. (Deuteronomy 12:11 emphasis added)*

A tithe is a tenth of personal income set apart as an offering to God or for works of mercy, and for the support of the church and the priesthood.

> *Thou shalt truly tithe all the increase of thy seed, that the field bringeth forth year by year. (Deuteronomy 14:22)*

And all the tithe of the land, whether of the seed of the land, or of the fruit of the tree, is the Lord's: it is holy unto the Lord. (Leviticus 27:30 emphasis added)

Bring ye all the tithes into the storehouse, that there may be meat in mine house, and prove me now herewith, saith the Lord of hosts, if I will not open you the windows of heaven, and pour you out a blessing, that there shall not be room enough to receive it. (Malachi 3:10 emphasis added)

And that we should bring the firstfruits of our dough, and our offerings, and the fruit of all manner of trees, of wine and of oil, unto the priests, to the chambers of the house of our God; and the tithes of our ground unto the Levites, that the same Levites might have the tithes in all the cities of our tillage. (Nehemiah 10:37 emphasis added)

The tithe is brought into the house of God, not any other place. That is your local church where you are fed. My pastor always says "You cannot eat at McDonald's and pay the bill to Whataburger." How true!

And I will rebuke the devourer for your sakes, and he shall not destroy the fruits of your ground; neither shall your vine cast her fruit before the time in the field, saith the Lord of hosts. And all nations shall call you blessed: for ye shall be a delightsome land, saith the Lord of hosts. (Malachi 3:11-12)

There are benefits of tithing:

1. The devourer is rebuked for your sake.
2. The fruit of your ground will not be destroyed.
3. Your vine will not cast her fruit before her time.
4. All the nations shall call you blessed.
5. You shall be a delight to the land.

> *Will a man rob God? Yet ye have robbed me. But ye say, Wherein have we robbed thee? In tithes and offerings. Ye are cursed with a curse: for ye have robbed me, even this whole nation. (Malachi 3:8-9 emphasis added)*

There are also consequences of not tithing:

1. You are regarded as a thief.
2. You are cursed with a curse.
3. You are not operating under open heavens.
4. You will fall before your enemy, the devourer.
5. You are a disobedient child.

When we honor the Lord with what we have, goodness and mercy will follow us all the days of our life and we will dwell in the house of the Lord forever. *"For where your treasure is, there will your heart be also" (Matthew 6:21).*

Offering is another way we bring our money into the house of the Lord to serve Him with our substance. An offering is something offered in worship or devotion, as to a deity; an oblation or sacrifice. It is a contribution given to or through the church for a particular purpose.

Let us consider for a moment the number of offerings in the Old Testament: Burnt, Meat, Sin, Trespass, Peace, Heave, and Drink offerings which were compulsory by the law given to Moses by God. I do not want to bore you with what each of them stand for, but the good news is that in the New Testament we are required not by law to give these offerings. What we are required to do is be grateful for what the Lord has done for us and sow bountifully.

Honour the Lord with thy substance, and with the firstfruits of all thine increase: So shall thy barns be filled with plenty, and thy presses shall burst out with new wine. (Proverbs 3:9-10)

But this I say, He which soweth sparingly shall reap also sparingly; and he which soweth bountifully shall reap also bountifully. Every man according as he purposeth in his heart, so let him give; not grudgingly, or of necessity: for God loveth a cheerful giver. And God is able to make all grace abound toward you; that ye, always having all sufficiency in all things, may abound to every good work. (2 Corinthians 9:6-8)

The story of Solomon explains the connection between our offering and the grace of God. After Solomon's offering, he had a visitation from God that changed his life forever. You can read the entire chapter of 1 Kings 3 to get the whole story, but this is how Solomon became the richest king the world had ever known.

And Solomon loved the Lord, walking in the statutes of David his father: only he sacrificed and burnt incense in high places. And the king went to Gibeon to sacrifice there; for that was the great high place: a thousand burnt offerings did Solomon offer upon that altar. In Gibeon the Lord appeared to Solomon in a dream by night: and God said, Ask what I shall give thee. (1 Kings 3:3-5)

Behold, I have done according to thy words: lo, I have given thee a wise and an understanding heart; so that there was none like thee before thee, neither after thee shall any arise like unto thee. And I have also given thee that which thou hast not asked, both riches, and honour: so that there shall not be any among the kings like unto thee all thy days. (1 Kings 3:12-13)

How Much is An Offering? The analogy given to us by Jesus should give us some clarity. Basically, it is according to what you have in your possession.

> *And Jesus sat over against the treasury, and beheld how the people cast money into the treasury: and many that were rich cast in much. And there came a certain poor widow, and she threw in two mites, which make a farthing. And he called unto him his disciples, and saith unto them, Verily I say unto you, That this poor widow hath cast more in, than all they which have cast into the treasury: For all they did cast in of their abundance; but she of her want did cast in all that she had, even all her living. (Mark 12:41-44)*

> *Every man according as he purposeth in his heart, so let him give; not grudgingly, or of necessity: for God loveth a cheerful giver. (2 Corinthians 9:7)*

The world system teaches us that we need to hold on to what we have so that we can have much at the latter end. God's system is contrary to that world's mindset. When you give your offering you are storing up for yourself in heaven.

> *But lay up for yourselves treasures in heaven, where neither moth nor rust doth corrupt, and where thieves do not break through nor steal: For where your treasure is, there will your heart be also. (Matthew 6:20-21)*

> *There is that scattereth, and yet increaseth; and there is that withholdeth more than is meet, but it tendeth to poverty. The liberal soul shall be made fat: and he that watereth shall be watered also himself. (Proverbs 11:24-25).*

Sacrificial giving is another way we bring resources to the

house of God. Sacrifice is to surrender or give up something of value to you. It was a big sacrifice in heaven when God decided to give us His only begotten Son. God will never ask us to do what He's not willing to do.

> *For God so loved the world, that he gave his only begotten Son, that whosoever believeth in him should not perish, but have everlasting life. (John 3:16)*

God appeared unto Moses and asked him to build a tabernacle where He may dwell. God had already given the children of Israel the ordinance about the types of offering He required of them. Then He wanted a tabernacle built. He gave Moses specific instructions for building this tabernacle. He wanted a sacrificial offering above all other offerings in order to build this tabernacle.

> *And let them make me a sanctuary; that I may dwell among them. According to all that I shew thee, after the pattern of the tabernacle, and the pattern of all the instruments thereof, even so shall ye make it. (Exodus 25:8, 9)*

> *And the Lord spake unto Moses, saying, Speak unto the children of Israel, that they bring me an offering: of every man that giveth it willingly with his heart ye shall take my offering. (Exodus 25:1, 2)*

> *And this is the offering which ye shall take of them; gold, and silver, and brass, And blue, and purple, and scarlet, and fine linen, and goats' hair, And rams' skins dyed red, and badgers' skins, and shittim wood, Oil for the light, spices for anointing oil, and for sweet incense, Onyx stones, and stones to be set in the ephod, and in the breastplate. (Exodus 25:3-7).*

David wanted to give sacrificially to God even though

God did not specifically ask this of him like He did Moses. He was able to do give sacrificially because he was already sold out for God. His heart was in the right place. When we understand that nothing belongs to us, then we are free to serve God with our substance like David.

> *Then David the king stood up upon his feet, and said, Hear me, my brethren, and my people: As for me, I had in mine heart to build an house of rest for the ark of the covenant of the Lord, and for the footstool of our God, and had made ready for the building. (1 Chronicles 28:2)*

> *But God said unto me, Thou shalt not build an house for my name,because thou hast been a man of war, and hast shed blood. (1 Chronicles 28:3)*

> *He gave of gold by weight for things of gold, for all instruments of all manner of service; silver also for all instruments of silver by weight, for all instruments of every kind of service. (1 Chronicles 28:14)*

> *All this, said David, the Lord made me understand in writing by his hand upon me, even all the works of this pattern. (1 Chronicles 28:19)*

> *And King David said to Ornan, Nay; but I will verily buy it for the full price: for I will not take that which is thine for the Lord, nor offer burnt offerings without cost. (1 Chronicles 21:24)*

OUR VOWS TO GOD

Another way we bring resources to the house of God is by paying the vows we have made to the Lord. A vow is a solemn promise, pledge or personal commitment, an act or a service. A vow is a solemn or earnest declaration.

And Moses spake unto the heads of the tribes concerning the children of Israel, saying, This is the thing which the Lord hath commanded. If a man vow a vow unto the Lord, or swear an oath to bind his soul with a bond; he shall not break his word, he shall do according to all that proceedeth out of his mouth. (Numbers 30:1, 2)

When thou shalt vow a vow unto the Lord thy God, thou shalt not slack to pay it: for the Lord thy God will surely require it of thee; and it would be sin in thee. But if thou shalt forbear to vow, it shall be no sin in thee. That which is gone out of thy lips thou shalt keep and perform; even a freewill offering, according as thou hast vowed unto the Lord thy God, which thou hast promised with thy mouth. (Deuteronomy 23:21-23 emphasis added)

It is quite obvious that vows are our proclamation to God. It is very important for us to guard our tongue in order not to say what we might not be able to do in God's presence. That does not mean only in the church. God's presence is everywhere, so be careful when you need something desperately and you begin to make deals with God.

Why do people make vows? People make vows when in need of something from God. God does not require us to make deals with Him, but if you tell God that you are going to do something when your prayer is answered, then please do it.

And when king Arad the Canaanite, which dwelt in the south, heard tell that Israel came by the way of the spies; then he fought against Israel, and took some of them prisoners. And Israel vowed a vow unto the Lord, and said, If thou wilt indeed deliver this people into my hand, then I will utterly destroy

> *their cities. And the Lord hearkened to the voice of Israel, and delivered up the Canaanites; and they utterly destroyed them and their cities: and he called the name of the place Hormah. (Numbers 21:1-3 emphasis added)*

> *And Jephthah vowed a vow unto the Lord, and said, If thou shalt without fail deliver the children of Ammon into mine hands, Then it shall be, that whatsoever cometh forth of the doors of my house to meet me, when I return in peace from the children of Ammon, shall surely be the Lord's, and I will offer it up for a burnt offering. So Jephthah passed over unto the children of Ammon to fight against them; and the Lord delivered them into his hands. (Judges 11:30-32 emphasis added)*

When we make our vows we need to watch how we make it. God will literally take you seriously.

> *And Jephthah came to Mizpeh unto his house, and, behold, his daughter came out to meet him with timbrels and with dances: and she was his only child; beside her he had neither son nor daughter. And it came to pass, when he saw her, that he rent his clothes, and said, Alas, my daughter! Thou hast brought me very low, and thou art one of them that trouble me: for I have opened my mouth unto the Lord, and I cannot go back. (Judges 11:34-35)*

When you pray and intend to make vow, it is not out of place to apply some wisdom and give yourself latitude to fulfill that which you have vowed.

> *And Jacob vowed a vow, saying, If God will be with me, and will keep me in this way that I go, and will give me bread to eat, and raiment to put on, So that I come again to my father's house in peace; then shall the Lord be my God: And this stone,*

which I have set for a pillar, shall be God's house: and of all that thou shalt give me I will surely give the tenth unto thee. (Genesis 28:20-22 emphasis added)

Hannah and Samuel

And she vowed a vow, and said, O Lord of hosts, if thou wilt indeed look on the affliction of thine handmaid, and remember me, and not forget thine handmaid, but wilt give unto thine handmaid a man child, then I will give him unto the Lord all the days of his life, and there shall no razor come upon his head. For this child I prayed; and the Lord hath given me my petition which I asked of him: Therefore also I have lent him to the Lord; as long as he liveth he shall be lent to the Lord. And he worshipped the Lord there. (1 Samuel 1:11, 27-28 emphasis added)

If we are believing and agreeing with God on a matter and make a vow in faith, I believe that the Lord of heaven will move on our behalf. If we make a vow when seeking God for promotion, to get a contract or for whatever need we have, God requires us to pay up. I also want to encourage us to write down anything we vow to God so that we don't forget.

God keeps his word; he expects us to keep ours.

My praise shall be of thee in the great congregation: I will pay my vows before them that fear him. (Psalm 22:25)

Offer unto God thanksgiving; and pay thy vows unto the most High: And call upon me in the day of trouble: I will deliver thee, and thou shalt glorify me. (Psalm 50:14-15)

Praise waiteth for thee, O God, in Sion: and unto thee shall the vow be performed. (Psalm 65:1)

Beloved, now are we the sons of God, and it doth not yet appear what we shall be: but we know that, when he shall appear, we shall be like him; for we shall see him as he is. (1 John 3:2)

KEY POINTS FROM PART TWO

- Studying the Word puts us in command of the world we live in.
- We cannot go wrong using God's words in our prayers and conversations with Him.
- Simple, heartfelt, full-of-faith prayers always get God's attention.
- Praise and worship are powerful tools that always bring the presence of God into any situation.
- Powerful praise brings powerful results.
- From now on there will be a "suddenly" in your vocabulary.
- When you praise God, there is always a commotion in the kingdom of darkness, and it always results into great victories and wholeness in your situation.
- A person with a servant's heart desires to serve others.
- People with servant's hearts are generally generous, humble, and become more faithful in their dealings with God.

PART THREE

N - NOTHING SHALL SEPARATE US FROM THE LOVE OF CHRIST

Now there was a day when the sons of God came to present themselves before the Lord, and Satan came also among them. And the Lord said unto Satan, Whence comest thou? Then Satan answered the Lord, and said, From going to and fro in the earth, and from walking up and down in it. (Job 1:6-7)

The thief cometh not, but for to steal, and to kill, and to destroy: I am come that they might have life, and that they might have it more abundantly. (John 10:10)

Looking at the scriptures above, it is very obvious that the devil's mission is to do whatever it takes to derail us from our walk with the Lord. Satan's Mission Statement is to steal, kill, and destroy our ability to live the kingdom lifestyle.

CHAPTER 6

UNDERSTANDING DISTRACTIONS

There are several things that can potentially derail us. Let us look at them one by one, so as to understand and guard against any distraction that might result in our derailment.

> *Who shall separate us from the love of Christ? Shall tribulation, or distress, or persecution, or famine, or nakedness, or peril, or sword? As it is written, For thy sake we are killed all the day long; we are accounted as sheep for the slaughter. Nay, in all these things we are more than conquerors through him that loved us. For I am persuaded, that neither death, nor life, nor angels, nor principalities, nor powers, nor things present, nor things to come, nor height, nor depth, nor any other creature, shall be able to separate us from the love of God, which is in Christ Jesus our Lord. (Romans 8:35-39)*

Tribulation simply means grievous trouble, a severe trial, or suffering. Tribulation comes because we have received the Word of God. The way to escape it is to stick to the

Word that brought the tribulation. Sounds ironic, but it is very true. We need to turn to God and obey His instruction and we will find our way out of our tribulation.

> *But if from thence thou shalt seek the Lord thy God, thou shalt find him, if thou seek him with all thy heart and with all thy soul. When thou art in tribulation, and all these things are come upon thee, even in the latter days, if thou turn to the Lord thy God, and shalt be obedient unto his voice. (Deuteronomy 4:29, 30)*

There are things that tribulations reveal in us. The quicker we develop these important characteristics, the quicker we graduate and move on to greater and better things in Christ.

> *And not only so, but we glory in tribulations also: knowing that tribulation worketh patience; And patience, experience; and experience, hope. (Romans 5:3-4 emphasis added)*

What is our disposition in tribulation? "Rejoicing in hope; patient in tribulation; continuing instant in prayer" (Romans 12:12). We are to rejoice and to continue in prayer, not to be discouraged knowing that God has already provided a way of escape. The Bible makes it clear that it is all worth it because we know the end from the beginning.

The earliest disciples experienced tribulation and we shall experience it, too, but in the long run we will have the victory in Jesus.

> *I, John, who also am your brother, and companion in tribulation, and in the kingdom and patience of Jesus Christ, was in the isle that is called Patmos, for the word of God, and*

for the testimony of Jesus Christ. (Revelation 1:9)

These things I have spoken unto you, that in me ye might have peace. In the world ye shall have tribulation: but be of good cheer; I have overcome the world. (John 16:33)

We are to count it all joy in tribulation, because we know the trying of our faith works patience in us and when patience does her perfect work in us, we will be perfect, whole, and wanting nothing.

DISTRESS AND PERSECUTION

Distress is defined as great pain, anxiety, or sorrow; acute physical or mental suffering, affliction, and trouble. To persecute means to pursue with harassing or oppressive treatment, especially because of religion, race or beliefs. It also means to annoy or trouble persistently. To fully understand distress and persecution we will look at a vivid example from the Word of God. One of many examples that came to mind is the story of Joseph. He was persecuted and in distress because of the vision God showed him about his future.

And Joseph dreamed a dream, and he told it his brethren: and they hated him yet the more. And he said unto them, Hear, I pray you, this dream which I have dreamed: For, behold, we were binding sheaves in the field, and, lo, my sheaf arose, and also stood upright; and, behold, your sheaves stood round about, and made obeisance to my sheaf. And his brethren said to him, Shalt thou indeed reign over us? or shalt thou indeed have dominion over us? And they hated him yet the more for his dreams, and for his words. And he dreamed yet another dream, and told it his brethren, and said, Behold, I have dreamed a dream more; and, behold, the sun and the moon and the eleven stars made obeisance to me. And he told it to his father, and to his brethren: and his father rebuked him, and said unto him, What is this dream that thou hast dreamed? Shall I and thy mother and thy brethren indeed come to bow down ourselves to thee to the earth? (Genesis 37:5-10)

Joseph invited persecution and distress into his life by sharing the vision God gave him about what was to come. Jacob, his father, sent him to go and see his brothers in the field. That was the opportunity his brothers were waiting for to prove if the word Joseph had said was from God and see if it would come to pass.

And when they saw him afar off, even before he came near unto them, they conspired against him to slay him. And they said one to another, Behold, this dreamer cometh. Come now therefore, and let us slay him, and cast him into some pit, and we will say, Some evil beast hath devoured him: and we shall see what will become of his dreams. (Genesis 37:18-20)

The purpose of persecution is to kill us so that the promise we have in the Word will not come to pass. Joseph's own brothers conspired to kill Joseph, but God intervened by persuading his brothers to do otherwise.

Like us, Joseph didn't know that when persecution comes it actually brings us closer to the fulfillment of the Word of God in our lives.

Come, and let us sell him to the Ishmaelites, and let not our hand be upon him; for he is our brother and our flesh. And his brethren were content. Then there passed by Midianites merchantmen; and they drew and lifted up Joseph out of the pit, and sold Joseph to the Ishmaelites for twenty pieces of silver:

and they brought Joseph into Egypt. (Genesis 37:27-28)

We know how his brothers lied about Joseph's death and sold him to slave traders going to Egypt. It seemed every time he thought his persecution or distress was over, there was another layer. However, it only meant he was getting closer to the fulfillment of the promise.

And the Midianites sold him into Egypt unto Potiphar, an officer of Pharaoh's, and captain of the guard. (Genesis 37:36)

We know God was with Joseph because everything he touched prospered. But apparently, Joseph's training for reigning was not yet complete, though, because God brought yet another round of distress and persecution into his life.

And it came to pass after these things, that his master's wife cast her eyes upon Joseph; and she said, Lie with me. But he refused, and said unto his master's wife, Behold, my master wotteth not what is with me in the house, and he hath committed all that he hath to my hand; There is none greater in this house than I; neither hath he kept back anything from me but thee, because thou art his wife: how then can I do this great wickedness, and sin against God? (Genesis 39:7-9)

This situation was trying, but Joseph refused to compromise God's standard. The result landed Joseph into prison, but again it was actually getting Joseph closer to the promise.

And it came to pass, when his master heard the words of his wife, which she spake unto him, saying, After this manner did thy servant to me; that his wrath was kindled. And Joseph's master took him, and put him into the prison, a place where the king's prisoners were bound: and he was there in the prison.

But the Lord was with Joseph, and shewed him mercy, and gave him favour in the sight of the keeper of the prison. (Genesis 39:19-21)

Doesn't it sound ironic that the word that brought the persecution and distress was the word that will bring deliverance once we are proven and tested? At this point, the baker and butler that worked for the king of Egypt ended up in the same prison with Joseph. This was all part of God's plan.

And it came to pass after these things, that the butler of the king of Egypt and his baker had offended their lord the king of Egypt. (Genesis 40:1)

And they dreamed a dream both of them, each man his dream in one night, each man according to the interpretation of his dream, the butler and the baker of the king of Egypt, which were bound in the prison. (Genesis 40:5)

The butler was restored and the baker was executed just as Joseph predicted through the interpretations of their dreams. Then Pharaoh had two dreams and the butler remembered Joseph. We know that from there God exalted Joseph to his rightful place as the second in command in all of Egypt. God had sent him there to save his family, the very ones who brought distress and persecution many years earlier on Joseph. However, the work that was done through all of these experiences had so developed Joseph's character that he became the ruler God wanted him to be in the kingdom.

Here are few scriptures to encourage us when we are going through persecutions and distress because of God's Word.

Blessed are they which are persecuted for righteousness' sake: for theirs is the kingdom of heaven. (Matthew 5:10)

Bless them which persecute you: bless, and curse not. (Romans 12:14)

Rejoice, and be exceeding glad: for great is your reward in heaven: for so persecuted they the prophets which were before you. (Matthew 5:12)

Yea, and all that will live godly in Christ Jesus shall suffer persecution. (2 Timothy 3:12)

Blessed are ye, when men shall revile you, and persecute you, and shall say all manner of evil against you falsely, for my sake. (Matthew 5:11)

I will lift up mine eyes unto the hills, from whence cometh my help. My help cometh from the Lord, which made heaven and earth. He will not suffer thy foot to be moved: he that keepeth thee will not slumber. (Psalm 121:1-3)

Persecutions and distress for the sake of the gospel bring out the best in us, so let us look up whenever we are persecuted or in distress for the Word's sake.

FAMINE, NAKEDNESS, PERIL, AND THE SWORD

And others were tortured, not accepting deliverance; that they might obtain a better resurrection: And others had trial of cruel mocking and scourging, yea, moreover of bonds and imprisonment: They were stoned, they were sawn asunder, were tempted, were slain with the sword: they wandered about in sheepskins and goatskins; being destitute, afflicted, tormented;

(Of whom the world was not worthy:) they wandered in deserts, and in mountains, and in dens and caves of the earth. And these all, having obtained a good report through faith, received not the promise: God having provided some better thing for us, that they without us should not be made perfect. (Hebrews 11:35-40)

Famine is an extreme and general scarcity of food. Nakedness is being without clothing and covering. Peril is exposure to injury, loss, destruction, grave risk, jeopardy, and danger. The sword is a weapon to symbolize military power, punitive justice, and authority. The best way to study this is to look at the life of the apostle Paul.

Are they ministers of Christ? (I speak as a fool) I am more; in labours more abundant, in stripes above measure, in prisons more frequent, in deaths oft. Of the Jews five times received I forty stripes save one. Thrice was I beaten with rods, once was I stoned, thrice I suffered shipwreck, a night and a day I have been in the deep; In journeying often, in perils of waters, in perils of robbers, in perils by mine own countrymen, in perils by the heathen, in perils in the city, in perils in the wilderness, in perils in the sea, in perils among false brethren; In weariness and painfulness, in watching often, in hunger and thirst, in fasting often, in cold and nakedness. If I must needs glory, I will glory of the things which concern mine infirmities. The God and Father of our Lord Jesus Christ, which is blessed for evermore, knoweth that I lie not. In Damascus the governor under Aretas the king kept the city of the Damascenes with a garrison, desirous to apprehend me: And through a window in a basket was I let down by the wall, and escaped his hands. (2 Corinthians 11:23-27, 30-33)

As it is written, For thy sake we are killed all the day long;

> *we are accounted as sheep for the slaughter. For I am persuaded, that neither death, nor life, nor angels, nor principalities, nor powers, nor things present, nor things to come, nor height, nor depth, nor any other creature, shall be able to separate us from the love of God, which is in Christ Jesus our Lord. (Romans 8:36, 38-39)*

Paul gives us good assurance that we are more than conquerors in Romans 8:37, "Nay, in all these things we are more than conquerors through him that loved us." Finally, I find 1 Corinthians 15:57-58 very comforting. "But thanks be to God, which giveth us the victory through our Lord Jesus Christ. Therefore, my beloved brethren, be ye steadfast, unmovable, always abounding in the work of the Lord, for as much as ye know that your labor is not in vain in the Lord."

CHAPTER 7

THE CONDITION OF OUR HEARTS

For us to live our lives well, we must also understand the condition of our heart where the Word of God is planted. To do this we need to consider different types of hearts and what the consequences are if our hearts are not right with God. There is a parable that will help us understand how important our heart condition is when it comes to making it in the kingdom where there is a living King. Our residency in the kingdom of God depends on our ability to retain the Word of God and have it available when we need it. Let us look at how the condition of ground or heart can affect us and can easily predispose us to trouble if our heart is not in the right place.

> *The sower soweth the word. And these are they by the way side, where the word is sown; but when they have heard, Satan cometh immediately, and taketh away the word that was sown in their hearts. (Mark 4:14-15)*

These people received the Lord as their Savior because

the Word was sown in their heart, but something happened immediately. Satan came along. However, they were deceived because Satan does not appear as someone with two horns on his head. It is important that we look at the forms in which Satan can manifest himself using his name as an acronym:

S - Socialization

A - Association and Attitude

T - Time Taker

A - Accountability

N - Neglect

SOCIALIZATION

Socialization is a continuing process whereby an individual acquires a personal identity and learns the norms, values, behaviors, and social skills appropriate to his or her social position. When an individual receives the Word, but continues in the social norms, values, and behaviors that do not conform to the Word of God, the impact of the Word will disappear very quickly. The continual process of acquiring personal identity that does not conform to the image of Christ will override their new identity in Him.

We must be careful not to conform to the lifestyle of the world once we have received the seed of truth from the Word of God.

> *And be not conformed to this world: but be ye transformed by the renewing of your mind, that ye may prove what is that good, and acceptable, and perfect, will of God. (Romans 12:2)*

ASSOCIATION AND ATTITUDE

To associate is to connect or bring into relation as thought, feeling, and memory. Who do you hang out with? Show me who you hang out with and who your closest friends are and I will show you who you are. Do you hang out with people that encourage you to go to church, study the Word, and pray? Or do you hang out with people that encourage you to do bad stuff?

Can two walk together, except they be agreed? (Amos 3:3)

Be ye not unequally yoked together with unbelievers: for what fellowship hath righteousness with unrighteousness? And what communion hath light with darkness? And what concord hath Christ with Belial? Or what part hath he that believeth with an infidel? And what agreement hath the temple of God with idols? For ye are the temple of the living God; as God hath said, I will dwell in them, and walk in them; and I will be their God, and they shall be my people. (2 Corinthians 6:14-16)

Your attitude is your manner, deposition, and feelings regarding the things of God. Your attitude will keep you in the kingdom if you embrace the Word of God.

For, brethren, ye have been called unto liberty; only use not liberty for an occasion to the flesh, but by love serve one another.

(Galatians 5:13)

TIME TAKER

We have been warned by the scripture about what to do with our time. Ecclesiastes 3:1 says, *"To everything there is a season, and a time to every purpose under the heaven."* However, if we do not use the time we are given wisely, we can find ourselves in trouble.

> *And it came to pass, after the year was expired, at the time when kings go forth to battle, that David sent Joab, and his servants with him, and all Israel; and they destroyed the children of Ammon, and besieged Rabbah. But David tarried still at Jerusalem. And it came to pass in an eveningtide, that David arose from off his bed, and walked upon the roof of the king's house: and from the roof he saw a woman washing herself; and the woman was very beautiful to look upon. And David sent and enquired after the woman. And one said, Is not this Bath–sheba, the daughter of Eliam, the wife of Uriah the Hittite? And David sent messengers, and took her; and she came in unto him, and he lay with her; for she was purified from her uncleanness: and she returned unto her house. (2 Samuel 11:1-4)*

We know the rest of the story, murder was committed, and an innocent child died in the process. The time kings go to war should not be a time to stay away from battle.

Sin will keep you longer than you are willing to stay, cost you more than you are willing to pay, and take you farther than you are willing to go.

> *Redeeming the time, because the days are evil. Wherefore be ye not unwise, but understanding what the will of the Lord is. (Ephesians 5:16, 17)*

ACCOUNTABILITY

What is it to be accountable to someone? It means we are

subject to and responsible to report, explain, and make ourselves answerable to someone. This is a difficult character trait to find among believers today, and that is the reason behind having so many weak brothers and sisters. We are not willing to look out for one another. For us to make it in the kingdom, we need to be accountable to someone who is not afraid of telling us the truth.

> *Confess your faults one to another, and pray one for another, that ye may be healed. The effectual fervent prayer of a righteous man availeth much. (James 5:16)*

NEGLECT

To neglect is not to pay attention to or pay too little attention to; disregard or slight; and to omit, through indifference or carelessness. One of the quickest ways to neglect your faith is to forsake the assembly of other people of God. The Bible encourages us to gather before the Lord because there are many tremendous rewards when we gather together in His name. However, if we neglect our love for God, we become lukewarm and God hates lukewarmness.

> *Not forsaking the assembling of ourselves together, as the manner of some is; but exhorting one another: and so much the more, as ye see the day approaching. (Hebrews 10:25)*
>
> *But they that wait (gather) upon the Lord shall renew their strength; they shall mount up with wings as eagles; they shall run, and not be weary; and they shall walk, and not faint. (Isaiah 40:31)*
>
> *How shall we escape, if we neglect so great salvation; which at the first began to be spoken by the Lord, and was confirmed unto us by them that heard him. (Hebrews 2:3)*

I know thy works, that thou art neither cold nor hot: I would thou wert cold or hot. So then because thou art lukewarm, and neither cold nor hot, I will spue thee out of my mouth. (Revelation 3:15, 16)

GUARD YOUR HEART

The need to guard our hearts cannot be overemphasized, because Satan always comes immediately after the Word of God is deposited in our hearts and tries to steal it away.

Keep thy heart with all diligence; for out of it are the issues of life. (Proverbs 4:23)

1. The Stony Ground

And these are they likewise which are sown on stony ground; who, when they have heard the word, immediately receive it with gladness; And have no root in themselves, and so endure but for a time: afterward, when affliction or persecution ariseth for the word's sake, immediately they are offended. (Mark 4:16-17)

This type of ground receives the Word with gladness, which means they were able to keep the Word for a while, but the Word had no root. Why did the Word fail to develop root? Jesus told His disciples a parable in Matthew 25:14-18 that will help us understand this principle.

For the kingdom of heaven is as a man travelling into a far country, who called his own servants, and delivered unto them his goods. And unto one he gave five talents, to another two, and to another one; to every man according to his several ability; and straightway took his journey. Then he that had received

> *the five talents went and traded with the same, and made them other five talents. And likewise he that had received two, he also gained other two. But he that had received one went and digged in the earth, and hid his lord's money. (Matthew 25:14-18)*

The only way to develop a root is to go out and trade with or use the deposit that the Word has made into us. How do we trade with and use what we have received? We need to develop a skill set by continually studying the Word. John the Beloved pointed out three categories of Christians (which parallels as stages of a believer's development):

- Little Children
- Young Men
- Father

Little children desire the milk of God's Word. Little children still talk about repentance from sin and other foundational principles. To grow as a new convert, we need to desire the sincere milk. In order to remain strong, we must drink a lot of milk. Staying planted in a local church is a key factor to developing a strong root.

> *My little children, these things write I unto you, that ye sin not. And if any man sin, we have an advocate with the Father, Jesus Christ the righteous: I write unto you, little children, because your sins are forgiven you for his name's sake. (1 John 2:1, 12)*

> *As newborn babes, desire the sincere milk of the word, that ye may grow thereby. (1 Peter 2:2)*

> *For every one that useth milk is unskillful in the word of righteousness: for he is a babe. (Hebrews 5:13)*

I have fed you with milk, and not with meat: for hitherto ye were not able to bear it, neither yet now are ye able. (1 Corinthians 3:2)

However, to develop our skills in the things of God, we must not stay at the milk level. Young men and fathers are to grow up and become teachers of the Word, not continue playing with the rudiments of our faith. Let us develop the talents that we have received from the Word sown into our hearts.

I write unto you, fathers, because ye have known him that is from the beginning. I write unto you, young men, because ye have overcome the wicked one. I have written unto you, fathers, because ye have known him that is from the beginning. I have written unto you, young men, because ye are strong, and the word of God abideth in you, and ye have overcome the wicked one. (1 John 2:13-14)

But strong meat belongeth to them that are of full age, even those who by reason of use have their senses exercised to discern both good and evil. (Hebrews 5:14)

Study to shew thyself approved unto God, a workman that needeth not to be ashamed, rightly dividing the word of truth. (2 Timothy 2:15)

Therefore leaving the principles of the doctrine of Christ, let us go on unto perfection; not laying again the foundation of repentance from dead works, and of faith toward God. (Hebrews 6:1)

For when for the time ye ought to be teachers, ye have need that one teach you again which be the first principles of the oracles of God; and are become such as have need of milk, and not of strong meat. (Hebrews 5:12)

The way to grow up in the Lord is to stay with the Word, "that he might sanctify and cleanse it with the washing of water by the word," (Ephesians 5:26), and to renew our mind, "and be not conformed to this world: but be ye transformed by the renewing of your mind, that ye may prove what is that good, and acceptable, and perfect, will of God" (Romans 12:2).

2. The Thorny Ground

And these are they which are sown among thorns; such as hear the word, and the cares of this world, and the deceitfulness of riches, and the lusts of other things entering in, choke the word, and it becometh unfruitful. (Mark 4:18-19)

The Word was equally sown to this type of ground, but there are three factors that choked the Word and it became unfruitful:

- Cares of this world
- Deceitfulness of riches
- Lusts of other things

The cares of the world are the essentials for our daily survival, but if we allow them to consume us we can easily be carried away, lose our footing, and the Word of God becomes unprofitable to us.

Therefore I say unto you, Take no thought for your life, what ye shall eat, or what ye shall drink; nor yet for your body, what ye shall put on. Is not the life more than meat, and the body than raiment? Therefore take no thought, saying, What shall we eat? or, What shall we drink? or, Wherewithal shall we be clothed? (For after all these things do the Gentiles seek:) for your heavenly Father knoweth that ye have need of all these things. (Matthew 6:25, 31-32)

This are the things that gentiles seek after and these things prevent them from coming to the house of God to fellowship. Please do not seek like the Gentiles do.

> *But seek ye first the kingdom of God, and his righteousness; and all these things shall be added unto you. (Matthew 6:33)*

> *Be careful for nothing; but in everything by prayer and supplication with thanksgiving let your requests be made known unto God. And the peace of God, which passeth all understanding, shall keep your hearts and minds through Christ Jesus. (Philippians 4:6, 7)*

Look at the example from one of Paul's fellow workers. A disciple named Demas was with other fellow laborers working for the Lord, but later in ministry he succumbed to the cares of the world.

> *For Demas hath forsaken me, having loved this present world, and is departed unto Thessalonica; Crescens to Galatia, Titus unto Dalmatia. Only Luke is with me. Take Mark, and bring him with thee: for he is profitable to me for the ministry. (2 Timothy 4:10, 11)*

May that not be your story.

3. The Good Ground

> *And these are they which are sown on good ground; such as hear the word, and receive it, and bring forth fruit, some thirtyfold, some sixty, and some an hundred. (Mark 4:20)*

The major difference in all these types of ground is the ability to bring forth fruit. If you look at the parable of the talent, God gave each individual according to their ability which played out in their productivity. The servant with five talents brought five more, the servant with two brought in two more, and the servant with one went and hid it. Our ability to produce results depends on the frequency and how skillful we are in our use of the Word. Let us look at few examples of people that received the Word on a good ground.

THE SPIES

> *And the Lord spake unto Moses, saying, Send thou men, that they may search the land of Canaan, which I give unto the children of Israel: of every tribe of their fathers shall ye send a man, everyone a ruler among them. And Moses by the commandment of the Lord sent them from the wilderness of Paran: all those men were heads of the children of Israel. (Numbers 13:1-3)*

Let's see the ones that received the Word in a good ground and the ones that received in one of those other types of grounds described earlier.

> *And Moses sent them to spy out the land of Canaan, and said unto them, Get you up this way southward, and go up into the mountain: And see the land, what it is; and the people that dwelleth therein, whether they be strong or weak, few or many; And what the land is that they dwell in, whether it be good or bad; and what cities they be that they dwell in, whether in tents, or in strong holds; And what the land is, whether it be fat or lean, whether there be wood therein, or not. And be ye of good courage, and bring of the fruit of the land. Now the time was the time of the first ripe grapes. (Numbers 13:17-20)*

> *And they returned from searching of the land after forty days. And they went and came to Moses, and to Aaron, and to all*

> *the congregation of the children of Israel, unto the wilderness of Paran, to Kadesh; and brought back word unto them, and unto all the congregation, and shewed them the fruit of the land. And they told him, and said, We came unto the land whither thou sentest us, and surely it floweth with milk and honey; and this is the fruit of it. (Numbers 13:25-27)*

After forty days they came back. They had an opportunity to see what the Lord had done in the wilderness and how the Lord delivered them from their various enemies. However, here is the surprising feedback from ten of the spies who went into the Promised Land.

> *Nevertheless the people be strong that dwell in the land, and the cities are walled, and very great: and moreover we saw the children of Anak there. The Amalekites dwell in the land of the south: and the Hittites, and the Jebusites, and the Amorites, dwell in the mountains: and the Canaanites dwell by the sea, and by the coast of Jordan. (Numbers 13:28-29)*

> *But the men that went up with him said, We be not able to go up against the people; for they are stronger than we. And they brought up an evil report of the land which they had searched unto the children of Israel, saying, The land, through which we have gone to search it, is a land that eateth up the inhabitants thereof; and all the people that we saw in it are men of a great stature. And there we saw the giants, the sons of Anak, which come of the giants: and we were in our own sight as grasshoppers, and so we were in their sight. (Numbers 13:31-33)*

Something must have happened to the Word and the deeds of the Lord recorded in their various hearts. Could it be that some of the things the Lord did fell by the way side of their hearts, or on the stony ground, or on the thorny ground? As we read this we see the more reason we need to guard our hearts and protect the good seed from the Word of God.

> *Wherefore let him that thinketh he standeth take heed lest he fall. (1 Corinthians 10:12)*

When Caleb and Joshua gave their reports, the people responded negatively. Because of that one incidence where the people chose not to receive the Word into good ground, they wandered for forty years in the wilderness

> *And Caleb stilled the people before Moses, and said, Let us go up at once, and possess it; for we are well able to overcome it. (Numbers 13:30)*

> *And Joshua the son of Nun, and Caleb the son of Jephunneh, which were of them that searched the land, rent their clothes. (Numbers 14:6)*

> *And the Lord's anger was kindled the same time, and he sware, saying, Surely none of the men that came up out of Egypt, from twenty years old and upward, shall see the land which I sware unto Abraham, unto Isaac, and unto Jacob; because they have not wholly followed me: Save Caleb the son of Jephunneh the Kenezite, and Joshua the son of Nun: for they have wholly followed the Lord. And the Lord's anger was kindled against Israel, and he made them wander in the wilderness forty years, until all the generation, that had done evil in the sight of the Lord, was consumed. (Numbers 32:10-13)*

We have the choice on what type of ground our heart is at any given time. Our obedience to the Word depends on how well we are keeping our hearts and which type of ground the Word of God is received.

Keep thy heart with all diligence; for out of it are the issues of life. (Proverbs 4:23)

KING SAUL AND AMALEK

Samuel also said unto Saul, The Lord sent me to anoint thee to be king over his people, over Israel: now therefore hearken thou unto the voice of the words of the Lord. Thus saith the Lord of hosts, I remember that which Amalek did to Israel, how he laid wait for him in the way, when he came up from Egypt. Now go and smite Amalek, and utterly destroy all that they have, and spare them not; but slay both man and woman, infant and suckling, ox and sheep, camel and ass. (1 Samuel 15:1-3)

Our obedience to the Word depends on which type of ground (our heart disposition) that received that particular instruction. Here Saul received the instruction from Prophet Samuel. It appears that Satan came and immediately removed the Word from his heart. We can say that his disobedience came from the state of his heart when the specific instruction was given to him.

And Saul smote the Amalekites from Havilah until thou comest to Shur, that is over against Egypt. And he took Agag the king of the Amalekites alive, and utterly destroyed all the people with the edge of the sword. But Saul and the people spared Agag, and the best of the sheep, and of the oxen, and of the fatlings, and the lambs, and all that was good, and would not utterly destroy them: but everything that was vile and refuse, that they destroyed utterly. (1 Samuel 15:7-9)

He took them for sacrifice unto The Lord. Yeah right? Can God not provide for Himself a lamb for sacrifice?" And Saul said unto Samuel, Yea, I have obeyed the voice of the Lord, and have gone the way which the Lord sent me, and have brought Agag the king of Amalek, and have utterly destroyed the Amalekites. But the people took of the spoil, sheep and oxen, the chief of the things which should have been utterly destroyed, to sacrifice unto the Lord thy God in Gilgal. (1 Samuel 15:20-21)

Then came the word of the Lord unto Samuel, saying, It repenteth me that I have set up Saul to be king: for he is turned back from following me, and hath not performed my commandments. And it grieved Samuel; and he cried unto the Lord all night. (1 Samuel 15:10-11)

That was how the kingdom of Saul came to an end. There are many stories in the Bible of people who followed the Lord to the end—the disciples in the New Testament, and Joseph in the Old Testament—to mention just a few. We have other people who did otherwise, like the story of Gehazi when Naaman came to see the prophet for healing. Obedience is better than sacrifice.

When we receive the Word of the Lord with a good heart, the result is always good.

Thy word have I hid in mine heart, that I might not sin against thee. (Psalm 119:11)

CHAPTER 8

DECEITFULNESS OF RICHES

For the love of money is the root of all evil: which while some coveted after, they have erred from the faith, and pierced themselves through with many sorrows. But thou, O man of God, flee these things; and follow after righteousness, godliness, faith, love, patience, meekness. (1 Timothy 6:10-11)

Money is a very important tool for the propagation of the gospel, so we need to have a lot of it. However, the deceitfulness of riches comes when things begin to possess us. The love of money is the root of all evil and can keep us from moving forward in our kingdom lifestyle as we see in the story of the rich young ruler. The best way to translate this is that his possessions had him. He wanted to inherit eternal life, but the deceitfulness of riches prevented him.

And a certain ruler asked him, saying, Good Master, what shall I do to inherit eternal life? And Jesus said unto him,

Why callest thou me good? None is good, save one, that is, God. Thou knowest the commandments, "Do not commit adultery, Do not kill, Do not steal, Do not bear false witness, Honour thy father and thy mother." And he said, "All these have I kept from my youth up." Now when Jesus heard these things, he said unto him, "Yet lackest thou one thing: sell all that thou hast, and distribute unto the poor, and thou shalt have treasure in heaven: and come, follow me." And when he heard this, he was very sorrowful: for he was very rich. (Luke 18:18-23)

THE PRODIGAL SON

A certain man had two sons: And the younger of them said to his father, Father, give me the portion of goods that falleth to me. And he divided unto them his living. And not many days after the younger son gathered all together, and took his journey into a far country, and there wasted his substance with riotous living. And when he had spent all, there arose a mighty famine in that land; and he began to be in want. And he went and joined himself to a citizen of that country; and he sent him into his fields to feed swine. And he would fain have filled his belly with the husks that the swine did eat: and no man gave unto him. (Luke 15:11-16)

After the one son got his money, he felt like he did not need the protection of his father's house any longer like many who leave the church for whatever reason. If you are reading this book and have found yourself out of fellowship because of the deceitfulness of riches, your Father's house is open. He is asking you to please come back.

THE LUST OF THE FLESH, THE EYES, AND THE PRIDE OF LIFE

Love not the world, neither the things that are in the world. If any man love the world, the love of the Father is not in him. For all that is in the world, the lust of the flesh, and the lust of the eyes, and the pride of life, is not of the Father, but is of the world. (1 John 2:15, 16)

Lust can easily derail our commitment to a kingdom lifestyle if care is not taken to stay on guard against them. Lusts can tempt us to do things we never imagined we would ever be doing. Let us look at some examples from the Bible.

KING AHAB AND NABOTH

And it came to pass after these things, that Naboth the Jezreelite had a vineyard, which was in Jezreel, hard by the palace of Ahab king of Samaria. And Ahab spake unto Naboth, saying, Give me thy vineyard, that I may have it for a garden of herbs, because it is near unto my house: and I will give thee for it a better vineyard than it; or, if it seem good to thee, I will give thee the worth of it in money. And Naboth said to Ahab, The Lord forbid it me, that I should give the inheritance of my father's unto thee. And Ahab came into his house heavy and displeased because of the word which Naboth the Jezreelite had spoken to him: for he had said, I will not give thee the inheritance of my fathers. And he laid him down upon his bed, and turned away his face, and would eat no bread. But Jezebel his wife came to him, and said unto him, Why is thy spirit so sad, that thou eatest no bread? And Jezebel his wife said unto him, Dost thou now govern the kingdom of Israel? arise, and eat bread, and let thine heart be merry: I will give thee the vineyard of Naboth the Jezreelite. So she wrote letters in Ahab's name, and sealed them with his seal, and sent the letters unto the elders and to the nobles that were in his city, dwelling with Naboth. And she wrote in the letters, saying, Proclaim a fast, and set Naboth on high among the people: And set two men, sons of Belial, before him, to bear witness against him, saying, Thou didst blaspheme God and the king. And then carry him out, and stone him, that he may die. (1 Kings 21:1-5, 7-10)

The elders of the city did exactly what she ordered and Naboth was killed. Ahab now had the perfect opportunity to take over the vineyard

And it came to pass, when Jezebel heard that Naboth was stoned, and was dead, that Jezebel said to Ahab, Arise, take possession of the vineyard of Naboth the Jezreelite, which he refused to give thee for money: for Naboth is not alive, but dead. And it came to pass, when Ahab heard that Naboth was dead, that Ahab rose up to go down to the vineyard of Naboth the Jezreelite, to take possession of it. And the word of the Lord came to Elijah the Tishbite, saying, And thou shalt speak unto him, saying, Thus saith the Lord, Hast thou killed, and also taken possession? And thou shalt speak unto him, saying, Thus saith the Lord, In the place where dogs licked the blood of Naboth shall dogs lick thy blood, even thine. (1 Kings 21:15-17, 19)

KING DAVID AND THE LUST OF THE EYES

And it came to pass, after the year was expired, at the time

when kings go forth to battle, that David sent Joab, and his servants with him, and all Israel; and they destroyed the children of Ammon, and besieged Rabbah. But David tarried still at Jerusalem. And it came to pass in an eveningtide, that David arose from off his bed, and walked upon the roof of the king's house: and from the roof he saw a woman washing herself; and the woman was very beautiful to look upon. And David sent and enquired after the woman. And one said, Is not this Bath–sheba, the daughter of Eliam, the wife of Uriah the Hittite? And David sent messengers, and took her; and she came in unto him, and he lay with her; for she was purified from her uncleanness: and she returned unto her house. And the woman conceived, and sent and told David, and said, I am with child. And David sent to Joab, saying, Send me Uriah the Hittite. And Joab sent Uriah to David. (2 Samuel 11:1-6)

The attempt to cover up his sin was a result of the lust of the eyes. When Uriah refused to go home to his wife, David took a drastic step to take care of the problem. However, the judgement of God came swiftly.

And David said to Uriah, Go down to thy house, and wash thy feet. And Uriah departed out of the king's house, and there followed him a mess of meat from the king. But Uriah slept at the door of the king's house with all the servants of his lord, and went not down to his house. And when they had told David, saying, Uriah went not down unto his house, David said unto Uriah, Camest thou not from thy journey? Why then didst thou not go down unto thine house? And Uriah said unto David, The ark, and Israel, and Judah, abide in tents; and my lord Joab, and the servants of my lord, are encamped in the open fields; shall I then go into mine house, to eat and to drink, and to lie with my wife? As thou livest, and as thy soul liveth, I will not do this thing. (2 Samuel 11:8-11)

And it came to pass in the morning, that David wrote a letter to Joab, and sent it by the hand of Uriah. And he wrote in the letter, saying, Set ye Uriah in the forefront of the hottest battle, and retire ye from him, that he may be smitten, and die. (2 Samuel 11:14-15)

Wherefore hast thou despised the commandment of the Lord, to do evil in his sight? thou hast killed Uriah the Hittite with the sword, and hast taken his wife to be thy wife, and hast slain him with the sword of the children of Ammon. Now therefore the sword shall never depart from thine house; because thou hast despised me, and hast taken the wife of Uriah the Hittite to be thy wife. Thus saith the Lord, Behold, I will raise up evil against thee out of thine own house, and I will take thy wives before thine eyes, and give them unto thy neighbour, and he shall lie with thy wives in the sight of this sun. For thou didst it secretly: but I will do this thing before all Israel, and before the sun. (2 Samuel 12:9-12)

There are numerous other examples in the Bible. Judas sold Jesus out for thirty shekels and Samson's problem was complicated because of the lust of other things. We need to guard against the works of the flesh at all cost.

And take heed to yourselves, lest at any time your hearts be overcharged with surfeiting, and drunkenness, and cares of this life, and so that day come upon you unawares. For as a snare shall it come on all them that dwell on the face of the whole earth. Watch ye therefore, and pray always, that ye may be accounted worthy to escape all these things that shall come to pass, and to stand before the Son of man. (Luke 21:34-36)

Now the works of the flesh are manifest, which are these; Adultery, fornication, uncleanness, lasciviousness, idolatry, witchcraft, hatred, variance, emulations, wrath, strife, seditions, heresies, envy, murders, drunkenness, reveling, and such like: of the which I tell you before, as I have also told you in time past, that they which do such things shall not inherit the kingdom of God. (Galatians 5:19-21)

KEY POINTS FROM PART THREE

- The earliest disciples experienced tribulations and we shall experience it, too, but in the long run, we will have the victory in Jesus.
- Persecutions and distress for the sake of the gospel brings out the best in us, so let us look up whenever we are persecuted or in distress for the Word's sake.
- Joseph didn't know that when persecution comes it actually brings us closer to the fulfillment of the Word of God in our lives.
- We must be careful not to conform to the lifestyle of the world once we have received the seed of truth from the Word of God.
- Sin will keep you longer than you are willing to stay, cost you more than you are willing to pay, and take you farther than you are willing to go.
- The need to guard our hearts cannot be overemphasized, because Satan always comes immediately after the Word of God is deposited in our hearts and tries to steal it away.

Kingdom Connection

- When we receive the Word of the Lord with a good heart, the result is always good.

PART FOUR

GO TO GOD FOR EVERYTHING

I am so delighted that we have come to letter "G" which stands for, "Go to God for Everything." We shall carefully study all we have to receive from Jesus our King in this part and as always, He is ready to help.

K - Know Him

I - Invest time in praise, prayer and fellowship

N - Nothing shall separate us from The Lord

G - Go to Him for everything

Where the word of a king is, there is power: and who may say unto him, What doest thou? (Ecclesiastes 8:4)

There hath no temptation taken you but such as is common to man: but God is faithful, who will not suffer you to be tempted above that ye are able; but will with the temptation also make a way to escape, that ye may be able to bear it. (1 Corinthians 10:13)

All things are delivered unto me of my Father: and no man knoweth the Son, but the Father; neither knoweth any man the Father, save the Son, and he to whomsoever the Son will reveal him. Come unto me, all ye that labour and are heavy laden, and I will give you rest. Take my yoke upon you, and learn of me; for I am meek and lowly in heart: and ye shall find rest unto your souls. For my yoke is easy, and my burden is light. (Matthew 11:27-30)

Therefore take no thought, saying, What shall we eat? Or What shall we drink? Or Wherewithal shall we be clothed? (For after all these things do the Gentiles seek) for your heavenly Father knoweth that ye have need of all these things. But seek ye first the kingdom of God, and his righteousness; and all these things shall be added unto you. (Matthew 6:31-33)

But my God shall supply all your need according to his riches in glory by Christ Jesus. (Philippians 4:19)

CHAPTER 9

HAVING OUR NEEDS MET

It is very important to establish the need for more of the revelation of Jesus in order to have our needs met as we live the kingdom lifestyle. All things are delivered to us through, Jesus, "the Author and Finisher of our faith" by the Father. Jesus is very willing to reveal the Father to us by the help of the Holy Spirit. Therefore, we must be able to follow instructions very carefully in order to secure our needs.

According to the scriptures, in order to come to Jesus for help we need to be laborers in His kingdom, and feel as though we are heavy laden. When we come to Him we are to take His yoke upon us and learn of Him. Jesus said when we do this He will give us rest. Rest is very important to God, because He knows when we take up His yoke then we are fully submitting ourselves to the understanding of His finished work.

There remaineth therefore a rest to the people of God. For he

> *that is entered into his rest, he also hath ceased from his own works, as God did from his. Let us labour therefore to enter into that rest, lest any man fall after the same example of unbelief. (Hebrews 4:9-11)*

We must have meekness and be lowly in heart to receive the rest and peace (shalom) of God—that means nothing broken and nothing missing. It is the peace and rest that can only come from God through Jesus Christ.

> *Be careful for nothing; but in everything by prayer and supplication with thanksgiving let your requests be made known unto God. And the peace of God, which passeth all understanding, shall keep your hearts and minds through Christ Jesus. (Philippians 4:6, 7)*

Though there are numerous needs and no two requests are the same among the children of God, we need to rest assured that Jesus has the answers for all. Any request that seems original to you, God has dealt with it for somebody in the kingdom before. So, you can relax because He's the expert in your particular situation. He can even do a new thing if it is needed.

> *The thing that hath been, it is that which shall be; and that which is done is that which shall be done: and there is no new thing under the sun. Is there anything whereof it may be said, See, this is new? It hath been already of old time, which was before us. (Ecclesiastes 1:9-10)*

> *Behold, I will do a new thing; now it shall spring forth; shall ye not know it? I will even make a way in the wilderness, and rivers in the desert. (Isaiah 43:19)*

> *There hath no temptation taken you but such as is common*

> *to man: but God is faithful, who will not suffer you to be tempted above that ye are able; but will with the temptation also make a way to escape, that ye may be able to bear it. (1 Corinthians 10:13)*

This is another Bible verse that should give us confidence along these same lines. The moment we get in trouble or in a difficult situation He goes into action right away, because He wants to give us rest. So, the next time you are in an unpleasant situation, look for the exit sign because He said with the temptation He also make a way of escape.

We can know that He hears us, all we have to do is ask in accordance with His will which is revealed in His Word.

> *And this is the confidence that we have in him, that, if we ask any thing according to his will, he heareth us: And if we know that he hear us, whatsoever we ask, we know that we have the petitions that we desired of him. (1 John 5:14-15)*

Before we look at the amazing works of God and how He has made provision for all our needs, He has one key word of advice for us.

> *Take therefore no thought for the morrow: for the morrow shall take thought for the things of itself. Sufficient unto the day is the evil thereof. (Matthew 6:34).*

The Lord's Prayer also makes it clear to us that we can ask God, *"Give us day by day our daily bread" (Luke 11:3).* So let us live our life without anxiety and with a full assurance that God is able to supply our daily needs. He is always mindful of our situation.

> *All things are delivered unto me of my Father: and no man knoweth the Son, but the Father; neither knoweth any man the Father, save the Son, and he to whomsoever the Son will reveal him. (Matthew 11:27).*

In the natural, it is quite obvious that the more I understand somebody the easier it is to get him or her to do what I am requesting of them. So, from the verse above we see that we do not know the Father except Jesus gives us the revelation of who God really His. Jesus was so intent on making sure His disciples understood this topic, that He said was going to do His best to explain it to them while He was with them. However, when He had to leave to go back to heaven, He told them He would ask the Father to send someone to them who would continue to remind them of what He had said and give even more revelation of Jesus and God the Father.

> *These things have I spoken unto you, being yet present with you. But the Comforter, which is the Holy Ghost, whom the Father will send in my name, he shall teach you all things, and bring all things to your remembrance, whatsoever I have said unto you. (John 14:25-26)*

TAKE MY YOKE UPON YOU

What does it mean to take His yoke upon us? When we get the right answer to that question, we will know how easy it is to get our petitions answered. Matthew 11:27 provided us with the insight of what it means to take His yoke.

A yoke is a device for joining together a pair of draft animals, especially oxen. It usually consists of a crosspiece with two bow-shaped pieces, each enclosing the head of an animal. It is compared to a harness. A yoke is simply a device to connect two things together. So what is Jesus' yoke? Jesus used the word yoke to help us understand the importance of joining ourselves with the truth He's about to tell us.

This truth Jesus has for us is in regard to the crucifixion and the finished work He accomplished with His death and resurrection. Nothing can be taken away or added to it. So, if we understand that His death and resurrection has provided us with everything we need or might need in the future, then we get it. We need to yoke ourselves together with this truth. When Jesus said it is finished, He meant it is finished. He did not say it was finished. It will always be—present continuous, so the need you are going to have many years from now will be covered when it materializes by His finished work on the cross as well. That's why He could give up the ghost, He knew no stone had been left unturned.

> *When Jesus therefore had received the vinegar, he said, It is finished: and he bowed his head, and gave up the ghost. (John 19:30)*

Paul, an apostle of Jesus Christ, had a great understanding of that fact when he made this statement to the Corinthian church:

> *And I, brethren, when I came to you, came not with excellency of speech or of wisdom, declaring unto you the testimony of God. For I determined not to know anything among you, save Jesus Christ, and him crucified. (1 Corinthians 2:1, 2)*

Paul knew that if the church or a believer can be yoked to

that truth, the rest would be easy. He also understand that any struggle to please God is over if we can just accept the finished work of Jesus Christ.

I am crucified with Christ: nevertheless I live; yet not I, but Christ liveth in me: and the life which I now live in the flesh I live by the faith of the Son of God, who loved me, and gave himself for me. (Galatians 2:20)

LEARN OF HIM

What do we need to learn of Jesus? To learn means to acquire knowledge or a skill by study, instruction, or experience. When we learn from somebody, there are at least two objectives that we must accomplish. Therefore, we need to ask ourselves:

Why does He do what He does?

How does He do it?

The answer is found in Acts 10:38, "How God anointed Jesus of Nazareth with the Holy Ghost and with power: who went about doing good, and healing all that were oppressed of the devil; for God was with him." Jesus loves to do good. That was what led Him to the cross in the first place.

God is a good God. He wants to be good to us, we just need to let Him by accepting the finished work of His Son, Jesus. If we do then we are yoked with Him. The good news is that He has not stopped doing good. Here is an example of Jesus's goodness.

And he entered again into the synagogue; and there was a man there which had a withered hand. And they watched him, whether he would heal him on the Sabbath day; that they might accuse him. And he saith unto the man which had the withered hand, Stand forth. And he saith unto them, Is it lawful to do good on the Sabbath days, or to do evil? To save life, or to kill? But they held their peace. And when he had looked round about on them with anger, being grieved for the hardness of their hearts, he saith unto the man, Stretch forth thine hand. And he stretched it out: and his hand was restored whole as the other. (Mark 3:1-5)

For with God nothing shall be impossible. (Luke 1:37).

BY HIS ANOINTING

How does do it? The Bible says God anointed Jesus. Jesus did everything by the anointing from the Father, which we can now receive from His finished work.

And Jesus came and spake unto them, saying, All power is given unto me in heaven and in earth. (Matthew 28:18)

The Spirit of the Lord God is upon me; because the Lord hath anointed me to preach good tidings unto the meek; he hath sent me to bind up the brokenhearted, to proclaim liberty to the captives, and the opening of the prison to them that are bound; To proclaim the acceptable year of the Lord, and the day of vengeance of our God; to comfort all that mourn; To appoint unto them that mourn in Zion, to give unto them beauty for ashes, the oil of joy for mourning, the garment of praise for the spirit of heaviness; that they might be called trees of righteousness, the planting of the Lord, that he might be glorified. (Isaiah 61:1-3)

And it shall come to pass in that day, that his burden shall be taken away from off thy shoulder, and his yoke from off thy neck, and the yoke shall be destroyed because of the anointing. (Isaiah 10:27)

Every anointing that we need to solve our problems is present in Jesus. He has all the power in heaven and in earth; so, He has got that territory covered pretty well.

BY HIS COMPASSION

We must know and understand that before we came to Jesus, His compassion was already at work. When He sees us with our burden, He is moved towards us with compassion.

I have compassion on the multitude, because they have now been with me three days, and have nothing to eat. (Mark 8:2)

And Jesus went forth, and saw a great multitude, and was moved with compassion toward them, and he healed their sick. (Matthew 14:14)

So Jesus had compassion on them, and touched their eyes: and immediately their eyes received sight, and they followed him. (Matthew 20:34)

And Jesus, when he came out, saw much people, and was moved with compassion toward them, because they were as sheep not having a shepherd: and he began to teach them many things. (Mark 6:34)

And he took the seven loaves and the fishes, and gave thanks, and brake them, and gave to his disciples, and the disciples to the multitude. (Matthew 15:36)

> *And he took bread, and gave thanks, and brake it, and gave unto them, saying, This is my body which is given for you: this do in remembrance of me. (Luke 22:19)*

> *Then they took away the stone from the place where the dead was laid. And Jesus lifted up his eyes, and said, Father, I thank thee that thou hast heard me. (John 11:41)*

MEEK AND LOWLY IN HEART

> *Take my yoke upon you, and learn of me; for I am meek and lowly in heart: and ye shall find rest unto your souls. (Matthew 11:29 emphasis added)*

Meekness and lowly in heart speak about His attitude. He wants us to have this same attitude so that we can receive quickly from God. Meekness simply means to be humbly patient, overly submissive or compliant, tamed, gentle, and kind. A lowly in heart is humble in attitude, behavior or spirit, in station or nature. Let us look at this parable that Jesus told which I believe summarizes it all.

> *And he spake this parable unto certain which trusted in themselves that they were righteous, and despised others: Two men went up into the temple to pray; the one a Pharisee, and the other a publican. The Pharisee stood and prayed thus with himself, God, I thank thee, that I am not as other men are, extortioners, unjust, adulterers, or even as this publican. I fast twice in the week, I give tithes of all that I possess. And the publican, standing afar off, would not lift up so much as his eyes unto heaven, but smote upon his breast, saying, God be merciful to me a sinner. I tell you, this man went down to his house justified rather than the other: for every one that exalteth himself shall be abased; and he that humbleth himself shall be exalted. (Luke 18:9-14)*

Kingdom Connection

It is all about His finished work and has nothing to do with our righteousness.

CHAPTER 10

CONSPIRACY, BITTER SITUATIONS, AND DEMONS

Let us look into some different situations that require divine intervention and then learn how God dealt with those situations. Remember, there is nothing new under heaven. If He dealt with these things then, He can surely deal with them now. Are you dealing with conspiracy, bitter situations, or demons? God has the answer.

DANIEL

Conspiracy is an evil, unlawful, treacherous or surreptitious plan formulated in secret by two or more persons. It is a plot. In the story of Daniel we see how God reacts to conspiracy against His people.

> *It pleased Darius to set over the kingdom an hundred and twenty princes, which should be over the whole kingdom; And*

> *over these three presidents; of whom Daniel was first: that the princes might give accounts unto them, and the king should have no damage.*
>
> *Then this Daniel was preferred above the presidents and princes, because an excellent spirit was in him; and the king thought to set him over the whole realm. Then the presidents and princes sought to find occasion against Daniel concerning the kingdom; but they could find none occasion nor fault; forasmuch as he was faithful, neither was there any error or fault found in him. Then said these men, We shall not find any occasion against this Daniel, except we find it against him concerning the law of his God. (Daniel 6:1-5)*

There was a conspiracy against Daniel put together by the presidents and princes of the land because they were jealous of Daniel's favor with the king. They came to the king and suggested a law that they knew Daniel would never obey. However, the king did not know that it was a conspiracy against Daniel, the idea sounded good to him, so the king signed it into law.

> *Then these presidents and princes assembled together to the king, and said thus unto him, King Darius, live forever. All the presidents of the kingdom, the governors, and the princes, the counsellors, and the captains, have consulted together to establish a royal statute, and to make a firm decree, that whosoever shall ask a petition of any God or man for thirty days, save of thee, O king, he shall be cast into the den of lions. Now, O king, establish the decree, and sign the writing, that it be not changed, according to the law of the Medes and Persians, which altereth not. (Daniel 6:6-8)*

If there are ordinances being written against you for any

reason, the king might not be able to remove them, but Jesus is able to take care of them. When we become aware of any conspiracy against us, we sometimes wonder whether to sue or fight for ourselves. How we handle it can reveal where we put our trust. When Jesus said it is finished, He meant it was all finished! Where do you put your trust?

> *Blotting out the handwriting of ordinances that was against us, which was contrary to us, and took it out of the way, nailing it to his cross; And having spoiled principalities and powers, he made a shew of them openly, triumphing over them in it. (Colossians 2:14, 15)*

Daniel knew where to put his trust. He upped his praying time to three times a day instead of stopping it as commanded by the new law. He prayed and gave thanks for the anticipated deliverance God was going to grant him. Daniel's colleagues reported him to king and the judgement was handed down based on the law. Some of us are wandering why God did not deliver him before he went into the lion's den. God always has a purpose for everything He does in our lives.

> *Now when Daniel knew that the writing was signed, he went into his house; and his windows being open in his chamber toward Jerusalem, he kneeled upon his knees three times a day, and prayed, and gave thanks before his God, as he did aforetime. (Daniel 6:10)*

> *Then the king commanded, and they brought Daniel, and cast him into the den of lions. Now the king spake and said unto Daniel, Thy God whom thou servest continually, he will deliver thee. (Daniel 6:16)*

The king suddenly realized that it was a conspiracy and

couldn't even reverse his own order. However, when God intervened, the king turned on the conspirators. When God comes into your situation, He takes all the glory. No one else can take credit for the victory in your life.

> *Then the king arose very early in the morning, and went in haste unto the den of lions. And when he came to the den, he cried with a lamentable voice unto Daniel: and the king spake and said to Daniel, O Daniel, servant of the living God, is thy God, whom thou servest continually, able to deliver thee from the lions? Then said Daniel unto the king, O king, live forever. My God hath sent his angel, and hath shut the lions' mouths, that they have not hurt me: forasmuch as before him innocence was found in me; and also before thee, O king, have I done no hurt. (Daniel 6:19-22)*

> *And the king commanded, and they brought those men which had accused Daniel, and they cast them into the den of lions, them, their children, and their wives; and the lions had the mastery of them, and brake all their bones in pieces or ever they came at the bottom of the den. Then king Darius wrote unto all people, nations, and languages, that dwell in all the earth; Peace be multiplied unto you. I make a decree, That in every dominion of my kingdom men tremble and fear before the God of Daniel: for he is the living God, and steadfast forever, and his kingdom that which shall not be destroyed, and his dominion shall be even unto the end. He delivereth and rescueth, and he worketh signs and wonders in heaven and in earth, who hath delivered Daniel from the power of the lions. (Daniel 6:24-27)*

Your situation is not beyond God's control. Let God take it over and watch how He will deliver you just as He delivered the three Hebrew boys from another form of conspiracy in Daniel Chapter 3. God can and will deliver you from any form of conspiracy you might face in your life. In both stories, God did not only deliver His people, He dealt with the conspirators and brought salvation to a whole nation.

> *He answered and said, Lo, I see four men loose, walking in the midst of the fire, and they have no hurt; and the form of the fourth is like the Son of God. Then Nebuchadnezzar came near to the mouth of the burning fiery furnace, and spake, and said, Shadrach, Meshach, and Abednego, ye servants of the most high God, come forth, and come hither. Then Shadrach, Meshach, and Abednego, came forth of the midst of the fire. And the princes, governors, and captains, and the king's counsellors, being gathered together, saw these men, upon whose bodies the fire had no power, nor was an hair of their head singed, neither were their coats changed, nor the smell of fire had passed on them. Then Nebuchadnezzar spake, and said, Blessed be the God of Shadrach, Meshach, and Abednego, who hath sent his angel, and delivered his servants that trusted in him, and have changed the king's word, and yielded their bodies, that they might not serve nor worship any god, except their own God. Therefore I make a decree, That every people, nation, and language, which speak anything amiss against the God of Shadrach, Meshach, and Abednego, shall be cut in pieces, and their houses shall be made a dunghill: because there is no other God that can deliver after this sort. Then the king promoted Shadrach, Meshach, and Abednego, in the province of Babylon. (Daniel 3:25-30)*

Maybe you are not dealing with a conspiracy, but there may be a bitter situation in your life. Does God have a solution for that as well? Yes, He does. Take a look at the city in this story (which represents the lives of many in our society, and sad to say, many in the kingdom, as well). The city is pleasant to look at, like the outward appearance of many of us. Things look very attractive and everything seems to be under control, but truly the water is polluted and the ground is barren so nothing is growing.

The men of the city went to Elisha. The Lord does not treat symptoms and leave the root cause untouched. Elisha went to the source of the problem, so when it was fixed it stayed fixed until this day.

> *And the men of the city said unto Elisha, Behold, I pray thee, the situation of this city is pleasant, as my lord seeth: but the water is naught, and the ground barren. And he said, Bring me a new cruse, and put salt therein. And they brought it to him. And he went forth unto the spring of the waters, and cast the salt in there, and said, Thus saith the Lord, I have healed these waters; there shall not be from thence any more death or barren land. So the waters were healed unto this day, according to the saying of Elisha which he spake. (2 Kings 2:19-22)*

Maybe you are dealing with oppression, depression or some other mental situation. Is there any provision from God for these conditions? Yes, there is because demonic oppression bows to the presence of Jesus. If you make Jesus the focus of your life, and believe and accept the finished work of the cross, deliverance is just around the corner.

> *And when he was come out of the ship, immediately there met him out of the tombs a man with an unclean spirit, Who had his dwelling among the tombs; and no man could bind him, no, not with chains: Because that he had been often bound with fetters and chains, and the chains had been plucked asunder*

> *by him, and the fetters broken in pieces: neither could any man tame him. And always, night and day, he was in the mountains, and in the tombs, crying, and cutting himself with stones. (Mark 5:2-5)*
>
> *But when he saw Jesus afar off, he ran and worshipped him, And cried with a loud voice, and said, What have I to do with thee, Jesus, thou Son of the most high God? I adjure thee by God, that thou torment me not. (Mark 5:6, 7)*
>
> *For he said unto him, Come out of the man, thou unclean spirit. And he asked him, What is thy name? And he answered, saying, My name is Legion: for we are many. (Mark 5:8, 9)*

The reason this man was having this much trouble was because he had been over powered by the legion of demons. Why did Jesus ask for the name of this demon? I believe it was just to show us that we need a greater One on the inside of us to tackle this type of problem. However, Jesus is the name above all names.

With God on our side, who or what can stand against us?

> *Ye are of God, little children, and have overcome them: because greater is he that is in you, than he that is in the world. (1 John 4:4)*

GERGESENES

The legion yielded to the Commander-in-Chief, and were all destroyed in the swine nearby. It does not matter how many problems we have, Jesus is greater and lives inside of us.

> *And when he was come to the other side into the country of the Gergesenes, there met him two possessed with devils, coming out of the tombs, exceeding fierce, so that no man might pass by that way. And, behold, they cried out, saying, What have we to do with thee, Jesus, thou Son of God? art thou come hither to torment us before the time? And there was a good way off from them an herd of many swine feeding. So the devils besought him, saying, If thou cast us out, suffer us to go away into the herd of swine. And he said unto them, Go. And when they were come out, they went into the herd of swine: and, behold, the whole herd of swine ran violently down a steep place into the sea, and perished in the waters. (Matthew 8:28-32)*

Rest assured, the same Commander in Chief, Jesus the Living Christ, will do the same for you as He did for this troubled man!

CHAPTER 11

DEBT, TAXES, AND DISEASES

Thou wilt shew me the path of life: in thy presence is fullness of joy; at thy right hand there are pleasures for evermore. (Psalm 16:11)

Remember, the best way to have a request granted is for God to show us the path of life to take. Once we get that right, there will be plenty of joy and we will receive help that brings pleasure for evermore from His right hand. Are you in debt and about to lose everything? Is there any provision for that as well? Yes, there is, let's look at the Bible:

Now there cried a certain woman of the wives of the sons of the prophets unto Elisha, saying, Thy servant my husband is dead; and thou knowest that thy servant did fear the Lord: and the creditor is come to take unto him my two sons to be bondmen. (2 Kings 4:1)

We see here that the woman came to Elisha first. She did

not approach the bank for a loan, go for a debt consolidation, or file for bankruptcy. I am not saying any of these are wrong, but we need divine guidance to make the right move. She simply went to God in prayer and ended up with God's prophet, Elisha.

> *And Elisha said unto her, What shall I do for thee? Tell me, what hast thou in the house? And she said, Thine handmaid hath not anything in the house, save a pot of oil. (2 Kings 4:2)*

The woman came to Elisha with a request. Elisha response's was to ask her what she thought he could do for her. Elisha quickly realized that the woman was not asking for any kind of debt advice. She was actually asking for divine intervention. The next question the prophet asked her was what do you have in the house? Your miracle begins with what you already have in your house or in your hand. Look at Moses at the Red Sea asking God what to do. God's response was to ask him what was in his hand. When you go to God in prayer and ask for solution, He begins to give you specific instructions using what He has already provided you with. If you follow His instructions, even if you do not understand why, breakthrough is certain.

> *Then he said, Go, borrow thee vessels abroad of all thy neighbours, even empty vessels; borrow not a few. And when thou art come in, thou shalt shut the door upon thee and upon thy sons, and shalt pour out into all those vessels, and thou shalt set aside that which is full. So she went from him, and shut the door upon her and upon her sons, who brought the vessels to her; and she poured out. And it came to pass, when the vessels were full, that she said unto her son, Bring me yet a vessel. And he said unto her, There is not a vessel more. And the oil stayed. (2 Kings 4:3-6)*

The woman came back to the man of God for further instruction on what to do with the miracle that had just taken place. In this day and age when we see a mighty move of God, many begin to take matters into their own hands. That is why their miracles are short-lived.

> *Then she came and told the man of God. And he said, Go, sell the oil, and pay thy debt, and live thou and thy children of the rest. (2 Kings 4:7)*

From debt to retirement, God is in the business of doing good. Are you in tax debt? It looks like Jesus lived in America and knows about Uncle Sam when we look at Matthew 17:24-26.

> *And when they were come to Capernaum, they that received tribute money came to Peter, and said, Doth not your master pay tribute? He saith, Yes. And when he was come into the house, Jesus prevented him, saying, What thinkest thou, Simon? Of whom do the kings of the earth take custom or tribute? Of their own children, or of strangers? Peter saith unto him, Of strangers. Jesus saith unto him, Then are the children free. Notwithstanding, lest we should offend them, go thou to the sea, and cast an hook, and take up the fish that first cometh up; and when thou hast opened his mouth, thou shalt find a piece of money: that take, and give unto them for me and thee. (Matthew 17:24-27)*

If you have tax issue going on, Jesus can provide a dramatic debt cancellation that is beyond your comprehension. The key in this verse is to trust the Lord, because the arm of flesh shall fail.

> *Thou wilt keep him in perfect peace, whose mind is stayed on thee: because he trusteth in thee. Trust ye in the Lord forever:*

> *for in the Lord Jehovah is everlasting strength. (Isaiah 26:3-4 emphasis added)*

Are you in need of divine provision? Does it seem like there is no way out of your dire situation? Does God have an answer for that?

> *And there was a great famine in Samaria: and, behold, they besieged it, until an ass's head was sold for fourscore pieces of silver, and the fourth part of a cab of dove's dung for five pieces of silver. (2 Kings 6:25)*

2 Kings 6:26-29 relates a horrible story as a result of this famine. The king took a drastic step and sent for the man of God, Elisha. Elisha quickly realizes that the king wanted God's intervention, so Elisha swung into action and made a proclamation that it can only take God to provide and meet that need. Here is good lesson for us to learn: Elisha was a man like us, yet he made a declaration that only God can back up. So when we are in any situation like this, ask for only things God can do, not what you can make happen or your friends can provide. The moral of this is that when you are in any situation, always ask for bigger and better things.

> *Then Elisha said, Hear ye the word of the Lord; Thus saith the Lord, Tomorrow about this time shall a measure of fine flour be sold for a shekel, and two measures of barley for a shekel, in the gate of Samaria. (2 Kings 7:1)*

How can this be possible, yesterday people were eating each other's kids and today there will be a surplus and everything will be in abundance? Even the king's right hand man questioned the possibility of that provision.

> *Then a lord on whose hand the king leaned answered the man of God, and said, Behold, if the Lord would make windows in heaven, might this thing be? And he said, Behold, thou shalt see it with thine eyes, but shalt not eat thereof. (2 Kings 7:2)*

Before Elisha spoke, God had already made a provision to meet that need and this is how God did it.

> *And there were four leprous men at the entering in of the gate: and they said one to another, Why sit we here until we die? If we say, We will enter into the city, then the famine is in the city, and we shall die there: and if we sit still here, we die also. Now therefore come, and let us fall unto the host of the Syrians: if they save us alive, we shall live; and if they kill us, we shall but die. And they rose up in the twilight, to go unto the camp of the Syrians: and when they were come to the uttermost part of the camp of Syria, behold, there was no man there. For the Lord had made the host of the Syrians to hear a noise of chariots, and a noise of horses, even the noise of a great host: and they said one to another, Lo, the king of Israel hath hired against us the kings of the Hittites, and the kings of the Egyptians, to come upon us. Wherefore they arose and fled in the twilight, and left their tents, and their horses, and their asses, even the camp as it was, and fled for their life. And when these lepers came to the uttermost part of the camp, they went into one tent, and did eat and drink, and carried thence silver, and gold, and raiment, and went and hid it; and came again, and entered into another tent, and carried thence also, and went and hid it. Then they said one to another, We do not well: this day is a day of good tidings, and we hold our peace: if we tarry till the morning light, some mischief will come upon us: now therefore come, that we may go and tell the king's household. (2 Kings 7:3-9)*

God will help you to identify your destiny helpers no matter what they look like when they bring your answers from heaven. Remember, it was four lepers that brought in the good tidings the entire nation was waiting for in this story.

The Lord is in the business of doing good.

> *Wherefore he saith, When he ascended up on high, he led captivity captive, and gave gifts unto men. (Ephesians 4:8).*

Are you in need of healing for a skin disease? Does God have a solution to that? Yes, He does. Let's look at another example in the Bible

> *Now Naaman, captain of the host of the king of Syria, was a great man with his master, and honourable, because by him the Lord had given deliverance unto Syria: he was also a mighty man in valour, but he was a leper. (2 Kings 5:1)*

Leprosy is a chronic, mildly infectious disease caused by mycobacterium leprae, affecting the peripheral nervous system, skin, nasal mucosa, and characterized by ulcerations, tubercular nodules, and loss of sensation that sometimes leads to traumatic amputation of the anesthetized part. Believe me people of God, He is the best dermatologist out there. He specializes in any kind of skin disease. There was a maid that was taken captive from Israel who gave valuable advice to her mistress that no amount of money could buy.

> *And the Syrians had gone out by companies, and had brought away captive out of the land of Israel a little maid; and she waited on Naaman's wife. And she said unto her mistress, Would God my lord were with the prophet that is in Samaria!*

for he would recover him of his leprosy. (2 Kings 5:2, 3).

The advice was for Naaman to seek God for his skin condition. I know we have the best of doctors in America, even skin specialists and dermatologists. I know that with Naaman he must have sought after the best of doctors in his day. I am not saying that seeing a doctor is bad, but seeking God is the first thing we should do.

And he brought the letter to the king of Israel, saying, Now when this letter is come unto thee, behold, I have therewith sent Naaman my servant to thee, that thou mayest recover him of his leprosy. And it came to pass, when the king of Israel had read the letter, that he rent his clothes, and said, Am I God, to kill and to make alive, that this man doth send unto me to recover a man of his leprosy? Wherefore consider, I pray you, and see how he seeketh a quarrel against me. (2 Kings 5:6-7)

Maybe it is time to showcase your God. Maybe you don't have any skin disease, but your friend, co-worker or a neighbor comes to you and says, "I know your God can help me" like a letter was brought to the king in this story. What are you going to do? We have so many opportunities to showcase our God, but we don't do it because we are afraid that the miracle will not happen. My advice is if he or she has the disease already, pray. If nothing happens, the worst case scenario is that he or she will make fun of you. What if something happens and the person receives their healing? Please consider that and reach out.

And it was so, when Elisha the man of God had heard that the king of Israel had rent his clothes, that he sent to the king, saying, Wherefore hast thou rent thy clothes? let him come now to me, and he shall know that there is a prophet in Israel. So

Naaman came with his horses and with his chariot, and stood at the door of the house of Elisha. (2 Kings 5:8, 9)

When you come to God for a solution and He gives you simple instructions, following those instructions always bring divine intervention.

Sometimes when divine instruction comes it does not settle well with our physical understanding. Some have lost out on what God intended to do because they are afraid to try something they do not understand. Thank God for friends that will encourage you to follow through with the will of God.

And Elisha sent a messenger unto him, saying, Go and wash in Jordan seven times, and thy flesh shall come again to thee, and thou shalt be clean. But Naaman was wroth, and went away, and said, Behold, I thought, He will surely come out to me, and stand, and call on the name of the Lord his God, and strike his hand over the place, and recover the leper. Are not Abana and Pharpar, rivers of Damascus, better than all the waters of Israel? May I not wash in them, and be clean? So he turned and went away in a rage.

And his servants came near, and spake unto him, and said, My father, if the prophet had bid thee do some great thing, wouldest thou not have done it? How much rather then, when he saith to thee, Wash, and be clean? Then went he down, and dipped himself seven times in Jordan, according to the saying of the man of God: and his flesh came again like unto the flesh of a little child, and he was clean. (2 Kings 5:10-14)

Lastly, he came back to the man of God. Some of us, when we receive our miracle, we don't even bother to share the testimony or come back to thank those who prayed for us. I pray today that you will share your testimony and that it will remind people that there is still a God who rules in the affairs of men.

> *And he returned to the man of God, he and all his company, and came, and stood before him: and he said, Behold, now I know that there is no God in all the earth, but in Israel: now therefore, I pray thee, take a blessing of thy servant. (2 Kings 5:15)*

CHAPTER 12

GOD BRINGS THE VICTORY

Are you in agony because of a great loss of property or investment? Does God care about that? Can God help with that? God says, "Call unto me, and I will answer thee, and shew thee great and mighty things, which thou knowest not" (Jeremiah 33:3). He is always with us and desires that we stop and take the time to call out to Him in our time of need, so He can not only bless us, but show great and mighty things above what we could have ever imagined.

The sons of the prophet asked Elisha to go with them to cut some trees to expand their dwelling in their time of need and he agreed to go. They understood the need for the presence of God to always be with them no matter what they were going to do.

> *And the sons of the prophets said unto Elisha, Behold now, the place where we dwell with thee is too strait for us. Let us go, we pray thee, unto Jordan, and take thence every man a*

> *beam, and let us make us a place there, where we may dwell. And he answered, Go ye. And one said, Be content, I pray thee, and go with thy servants. And he answered, I will go. So he went with them. And when they came to Jordan, they cut down wood. But as one was felling a beam, the axe head fell into the water: and he cried, and said, Alas, master! For it was borrowed. (2 Kings 6:1-5)*

The axe head they were working with fell into the water—and it was borrowed (and that makes it a great loss). How many times do we lose money, houses, cars or other properties that we secured a loan to buy? Like these men trying to expand their housing, God's divine intervention may be needed in your life as well to achieve the victory over your situation.

> *And the man of God said, Where fell it? And he shewed him the place. And he cut down a stick, and cast it in thither; and the iron did swim. Therefore said he, Take it up to thee. And he put out his hand, and took it. (2 Kings 6:6-7)*

God is asking you today where and when did you suffer your loss? Please know that if there is a need for divine intervention, you will not be able to figure out how the recovery is going to come. Do not try to figure Him out, because you cannot. Just reach in and get your stuff back upon His command. However, if you do not ask, you will not receive. The day you bring your request about your losses to God, is the day you will have your joy to the max. Whatever you are in need of, God will divinely intervene in Jesus' name if you will but ask. The Lord will restore all your losses from your past now that you are in the kingdom.

> *And in that day ye shall ask me nothing. Verily, verily, I say unto you, Whatsoever ye shall ask the Father in my name, he*

> *will give it you. Hitherto have ye asked nothing in my name: ask, and ye shall receive, that your joy may be full. (John 16:23-24)*

> *And I will restore to you the years that the locust hath eaten, the cankerworm, and the caterpillar, and the palmerworm, my great army which I sent among you. And ye shall eat in plenty, and be satisfied, and praise the name of the Lord your God, that hath dealt wondrously with you: and my people shall never be ashamed. (Joel 2:25-26)*

RECEIVING THE PROMISES OF GOD

Are you very close to the fulfilment of a promise that you are trusting the Lord for and it seems you are being blocked from receiving it? When you are sure of His promise then you need to ask God for divine instructions to get it.

> *Now Jericho was straightly shut up because of the children of Israel: none went out, and none came in. And the Lord said unto Joshua, See, I have given into thine hand Jericho, and the king thereof, and the mighty men of valour. (Joshua 6:1-2)*

God had given Jericho to Joshua and his followers. Joshua had the promise right in front of him, but he needed divine instruction from the One who gave him the promise. Some of us get a promise or are standing on a scripture, but then turn to others for instruction who have no idea how to get in instead of going directly to the Giver of the promise.

If we were faced with this kind of situation, our first thought would be to bring in a bobcat or a bulldozer to knock the wall down. We might ask everybody around us for advice on how to take down those walls. However, God is the one with the answer.

These people did exactly what the Lord asked of them and the result was amazing. From Joshua 6:6-14 it is obvious that it was done according to God's command. The result of that obedience is evident from verses 15-19. Then the Lord gave them more instruction which they followed as well.

> *And ye shall compass the city, all ye men of war, and go round about the city once. Thus shalt thou do six days. And seven priests shall bear before the ark seven trumpets of rams' horns: and the seventh day ye shall compass the city seven times, and the priests shall blow with the trumpets. And it shall come to pass, that when they make a long blast with the ram's horn, and when ye hear the sound of the trumpet, all the people shall shout with a great shout; and the wall of the city shall fall down flat, and the people shall ascend up every man straight before him.*
>
> *And Joshua the son of Nun called the priests, and said unto them, Take up the ark of the covenant, and let seven priests bear seven trumpets of rams' horns before the ark of the Lord. And he said unto the people, Pass on, and compass the city, and let him that is armed pass on before the ark of the Lord. And it came to pass, when Joshua had spoken unto the people, that the seven priests bearing the seven trumpets of rams' horns passed on before the Lord, and blew with the trumpets: and the ark of the covenant of the Lord followed them. And the armed men went before the priests that blew with the trumpets, and the reward came after the ark, the priests going on, and blowing with the trumpets. And Joshua had commanded the people, saying, Ye shall not shout, nor make any noise with*

> *your voice, neither shall any word proceed out of your mouth, until the day I bid you shout; then shall ye shout. So the ark of the Lord compassed the city, going about it once: and they came into the camp, and lodged in the camp. And Joshua rose early in the morning, and the priests took up the ark of the Lord. And seven priests bearing seven trumpets of rams' horns before the ark of the Lord went on continually, and blew with the trumpets: and the armed men went before them; but the rereward came after the ark of the Lord, the priests going on, and blowing with the trumpets. And the second day they compassed the city once, and returned into the camp: so they did six days.*
>
> *And it came to pass on the seventh day, that they rose early about the dawning of the day, and compassed the city after the same manner seven times: only on that day they compassed the city seven times. And it came to pass at the seventh time, when the priests blew with the trumpets, Joshua said unto the people, Shout; for the Lord hath given you the city. And the city shall be accursed, even it, and all that are therein, to the Lord: only Rahab the harlot shall live, she and all that are with her in the house, because she hid the messengers that we sent. And ye, in any wise keep yourselves from the accursed thing, lest ye make yourselves accursed, when ye take of the accursed thing, and make the camp of Israel a curse, and trouble it. But all the silver, and gold, and vessels of brass and iron, are consecrated unto the Lord: they shall come into the treasury of the Lord. (Joshua 6:3-19 emphasis added)*

Let us look at the instructions God gave to His people so they could receive their promise:

1. Take up the ark of covenant. The Word is the key to your victory, look for what God has said regarding

your situation and take it up.

2. You shall not shout, nor make any noise, neither shall any word proceed out of your mouth, until the day I bid you shout. God wants you to be still and to say nothing about your problems contrary to His promise.

3. Go around it once a day for six days. God could have done it on the first day, obedience is the key word. What is God telling you about your situation?

4. Seven times on the seventh day. When God gives us victory it is perfect, this simply symbolizes Jubilee. In Jubilee there is a complete release and victory.

5. Then shout on the seventh day. Rejoice when your victory is accomplished. Some of us like to give testimony about every step God is taking us through with our situation thereby causing a further delay. Mary kept the story of having our Messiah until it was accomplished.

> *So the people shouted when the priests blew with the trumpets: and it came to pass, when the people heard the sound of the trumpet, and the people shouted with a great shout, that the wall fell down flat, so that the people went up into the city, every man straight before him, and they took the city. And they utterly destroyed all that was in the city, both man and woman, young and old, and ox, and sheep, and ass, with the edge of the sword. (Joshua 6:20, 21).*

Our God is still in the business of bringing down walls today.

All we need to do is obey the instructions that are given to us. When He gives us a promise, God cannot lie. He has promised us He has plans for us that are good. He wants us to enjoy the rest of our life manifesting His kingdom lifestyle. He also wants us to look forward to our growing relationship with Him with great excitement.

> *Heaven and earth shall pass away, but my words shall not pass away. (Matthew 24:35)*

> *For I know the thoughts that I think toward you, saith the Lord, thoughts of peace, and not of evil, to give you an expected end. (Jeremiah 29:11)*

WAITING FOR THE BLESSING OF THE LORD

> *Now there was a certain man of Ramathaim–zophim, of mount Ephraim, and his name was Elkanah, the son of Jeroham, the son of Elihu, the son of Tohu, the son of Zuph, an Ephrathite: And he had two wives; the name of the one was Hannah, and the name of the other Peninnah: and Peninnah had children, but Hannah had no children. And this man went up out of his city yearly to worship and to sacrifice unto the Lord of hosts in Shiloh. And the two sons of Eli, Hophni and Phinehas, the priests of the Lord, were there. (1 Samuel 1:1-3)*

> *And as he did so year by year, when she went up to the house of the Lord, so she provoked her; therefore she wept, and did not eat. (1 Samuel 1:7)*

The man in this story takes his wives and goes to be in God's presence every year. Every year, Hannah, one of his wives, asks him to go before the Lord and ask for her to conceive and bear a child. She continues to go with her husband despite the fact that she has not received what she wanted from the Lord. One year, Hannah decided to change her status by asking the Lord directly for a child.

> *And she was in bitterness of soul, and prayed unto the Lord, and wept sore. And she vowed a vow, and said, O Lord of hosts, if thou wilt indeed look on the affliction of thine handmaid, and remember me, and not forget thine handmaid, but wilt give unto thine handmaid a man child, then I will give him unto the Lord all the days of his life, and there shall no razor come upon his head. (1 Samuel 1:10-11)*

> *Now Hannah, she spake in her heart; only her lips moved, but her voice was not heard: therefore Eli thought she had been drunken. And Hannah answered and said, No, my lord, I am a woman of a sorrowful spirit: I have drunk neither wine nor strong drink, but have poured out my soul before the Lord. Then Eli answered and said, Go in peace: and the God of Israel grant thee thy petition that thou hast asked of him. (1 Samuel 1:13, 15, 17)*

She prayed to the Lord and spoke her heart, but no words were spoken out loud so the priest that saw her thought she was drunk. Her response to the priest revealed the condition of her heart and the intensity of her prayer. The man of God told her to go in peace and that the God of Israel would honor that request.

> *Wherefore it came to pass, when the time was come about after Hannah had conceived, that she bare a son, and called his name Samuel, saying, Because I have asked him of the Lord. (1 Samuel 1:20)*

Whatever you are asking from the Lord that is according to His will shall be granted in Jesus name. If you are thinking that age is not on your side, look at Sarah who had Isaac at a very old age. Realize your solution is in the name of the Lord. It shall come to pass for you, if you will stand on His promises and patiently wait for His blessings.

There may be areas of your life that are barren, all you need to do is pray and ask the Lord for fruitfulness.

> *The Lord will perfect that which concerneth me: thy mercy, O Lord, endureth forever: forsake not the works of thine own hands. (Psalm 138:8)*

CHAPTER 13

REJECTION AND WILDERNESS TIMES

To be rejected hurts a lot and can be very lonely, but it is time to leave those hurts behind and move to the next level. Please do not hold on to what God has already dealt with for you. Are you being rejected by family members, friends, organizations or neighbors? It is God that will lift you up and make you relevant so that they will come to submit to you as you achieve your purpose in the kingdom of God.

> *The sons also of them that afflicted thee shall come bending unto thee; and all they that despised thee shall bow themselves down at the soles of thy feet; and they shall call thee, The city of the Lord, The Zion of the Holy One of Israel. Whereas thou hast been forsaken and hated, so that no man went through thee, I will make thee an eternal excellency, a joy of many generations. Thou shalt also suck the milk of the Gentiles, and shalt suck the breast of kings: and thou shalt know that I the Lord am thy Saviour and thy Redeemer, the mighty One of Jacob. (Isaiah 60:14-16)*

The story of David readily came to mind when thinking of this topic of rejection. David was the last kid in the family and was relegated to doing a lot of the dirty jobs that nobody else wanted to do. He was looked down upon by his brothers and apparently even his father, Jesse, as well. When Samuel came into the house looking for next king of Israel, Jesse, presented all of his sons but David

> *And he said, Peaceably: I am come to sacrifice unto the Lord: sanctify yourselves, and come with me to the sacrifice. And he sanctified Jesse and his sons, and called them to the sacrifice. And it came to pass, when they were come, that he looked on Eliab, and said, Surely the Lord's anointed is before him. But the Lord said unto Samuel, Look not on his countenance, or on the height of his stature; because I have refused him: for the Lord seeth not as man seeth; for man looketh on the outward appearance, but the Lord looketh on the heart. Then Jesse called Abinadab, and made him pass before Samuel. And he said, Neither hath the Lord chosen this. Then Jesse made Shammah to pass by. And he said, Neither hath the Lord chosen this. Again, Jesse made seven of his sons to pass before Samuel. And Samuel said unto Jesse, The Lord hath not chosen these. (1 Samuel 16:5-10)*

Let us look at a point here that is very crucial to receiving from the Lord. Samuel sanctified all of David's brothers, but that did not make them qualified for elevation.

PROMOTION COMES ONLY FROM GOD

> *So then it is not of him that willeth, nor of him that runneth, but of God that sheweth mercy. (Romans 9:16)*

> *I returned, and saw under the sun, that the race is not to the*

> *swift, nor the battle to the strong, neither yet bread to the wise, nor yet riches to men of understanding, nor yet favour to men of skill; but time and chance happeneth to them all. (Ecclesiastes 9:11)*

David was never thought of or even mentioned when Samuel asked to see all of the sons of Jesse. So Samuel, under the unction of the Almighty, asked Jesse if he had brought forward all of his children.

> *And Samuel said unto Jesse, Are here all thy children? And he said, There remaineth yet the youngest, and, behold, he keepeth the sheep. And Samuel said unto Jesse, Send and fetch him: for we will not sit down till he come hither. (1 Samuel 16:11)*

Samuel said they would not sit down until David was brought before him. God Himself sought out the one that was forgotten by everybody else, and when David came in, the prophet anointed him as the next king of Israel. The Lord told Samuel this was the one He had chosen. The Spirit of the Lord came upon David from that day forward.

> *And he sent, and brought him in. Now he was ruddy, and withal of a beautiful countenance, and goodly to look to. And the Lord said, Arise, anoint him: for this is he. Then Samuel took the horn of oil, and anointed him in the midst of his brethren: and the Spirit of the Lord came upon David from that day forward. So Samuel rose up, and went to Ramah. (1 Samuel 16:12-13)*

Every burden and yoke that may have caused you to be rejected, forsaken, and passed over many times for promotion, will be broken and destroyed by the anointing in the name of Jesus.

> *And it shall come to pass in that day, that his burden shall be taken away from off thy shoulder, and his yoke from off thy neck, and the yoke shall be destroyed because of the anointing. (Isaiah 10:27)*

Let's look at what the anointing did for the once forgotten, rejected son. He became the leader over all of those who rejected him.

> *David therefore departed thence, and escaped to the cave Adullam: and when his brethren and all his father's house heard it, they went down thither to him. And every one that was in distress, and every one that was in debt, and every one that was discontented, gathered themselves unto him; and he became a captain over them: and there were with him about four hundred men. (1 Samuel 22:1-2)*

Yes, Joseph's brothers hated him because of his dreams and ambition, but even more so because his father loved him. This was the main reason his brothers rejected him to the point of plotting his murder.

> *Now Israel loved Joseph more than all his children, because he was the son of his old age: and he made him a coat of many colours. And when his brethren saw that their father loved him more than all his brethren, they hated him, and could not speak peaceably unto him. (Genesis 37:3, 4)*

Now you can relate to this, especially if your rejection is simply because of the love God, your Father. Many will be jealous because you are favored despite the fact that they do not consider you a candidate for His blessings and love. Of course, we know that the other reason Joseph was severely rejected was that he dared to have a big dream or vision for his life

And Joseph dreamed a dream, and he told it his brethren: and they hated him yet the more. And he said unto them, Hear, I pray you, this dream which I have dreamed: For, behold, we were binding sheaves in the field, and, lo, my sheaf arose, and also stood upright; and, behold, your sheaves stood round about, and made obeisance to my sheaf. And his brethren said to him, Shalt thou indeed reign over us? or shalt thou indeed have dominion over us? And they hated him yet the more for his dreams, and for his words. And he dreamed yet another dream, and told it his brethren, and said, Behold, I have dreamed a dream more; and, behold, the sun and the moon and the eleven stars made obeisance to me. And he told it to his father, and to his brethren: and his father rebuked him, and said unto him, What is this dream that thou hast dreamed? Shall I and thy mother and thy brethren indeed come to bow down ourselves to thee to the earth? And his brethren envied him; but his father observed the saying. (Genesis 37:5-11)

It is high time to make your vision plain despite the fact that they will reject you, and even conspire against you. Remember, you need their conspiracy to help propel you toward your destiny. This is your appointed time for all that God has told you to come to pass.

And the Lord answered me, and said, Write the vision, and make it plain upon tables, that he may run that readeth it. For the vision is yet for an appointed time, but at the end it shall speak, and not lie: though it tarry, wait for it; because it will surely come, it will not tarry. (Habakkuk 2:2, 3)

And when they saw him afar off, even before he came near unto them, they conspired against him to slay him. And they said one to another, Behold, this dreamer cometh. (Genesis 37:18, 19)

Until they call you the dreamer or despise you because of your vision, your dream might not come true. Rejection usually leads you right into your destiny, so do not give up because the fulfilment of your dream is right around the next corner. It took thirteen years for Joseph to become the Prime Minister over Egypt and to step into all that God had purposed for him. Do not get intimidated because of rejection. It may be your appointed time, so wait for that change to come from the Lord.

And that, knowing the time, that now it is high time to awake out of sleep: for now is our salvation nearer than when we believed. (Romans 13:11).

If a man die, shall he live again? All the days of my appointed time will I wait, till my change come. (Job 14:14)

PROVISION DURING OUR WILDERNESS TIMES

Are you in need of a provision and it looks like that cannot be done because of your location? We have learned to look for our answers in the Bible, His written Word.

In Exodus we read how the children of Israel were in the wilderness and had seen many wonders the Lord had done for them. Suddenly, they were in need of food and they thought that because of their location it was going to be impossible for God to meet that need. The children of Israel then murmured against God.

And the children of Israel said unto them, Would to God we had died by the hand of the Lord in the land of Egypt, when we sat by the flesh pots, and when we did eat bread to the full;

for ye have brought us forth into this wilderness, to kill this whole assembly with hunger. (Exodus 16:3)

Then said the Lord unto Moses, Behold, I will rain bread from heaven for you; and the people shall go out and gather a certain rate every day, that I may prove them, whether they will walk in my law, or no. And it came to pass, that at even the quails came up, and covered the camp: and in the morning the dew lay round about the host. And when the dew that lay was gone up, behold, upon the face of the wilderness there lay a small round thing, as small as the hoar frost on the ground. And when the children of Israel saw it, they said one to another, It is manna: for they wist not what it was. And Moses said unto them, This is the bread which the Lord hath given you to eat. (Exodus 16:4, 13-15)

I believe if the children of Israel had asked the Lord through Moses, God would have provided for them. After all, He had given them a pillar of fire by night and a pillar of cloud by day to guide them in the way they should go. This simply tells us that we should not take God for granted. He wants to provide for us and has told us how to seek His provision, but He also hears us when we utter our discontentment. That murmuring generation all died in the wilderness because of their unbelief—all of them, except Joshua and Caleb. A good lesson for us is not to forget the goodness of the Lord.

Are you in a wilderness at this stage of your life, wondering where the next breakthrough is coming from? Don't murmur. What is murmuring? It is a mumbled or private expression of discontent. When you murmur instead of asking God for your need, you might not like what you get.

Kingdom Connection

The Lord is able to supply all our needs irrespective of our location. We do not want to receive from the Lord, forget His provision, murmur about what we do not have, and as a result die in the wilderness before we reach our Promised Land. The Israelites were on their way to the Promise Land but they missed out on it for being ungrateful, and murmuring and complaining about what they did not have instead of thanking Him for what He had provided for them. Please make sure you make it to your Promised Land.

> *And Jabez called on the God of Israel, saying, Oh that thou wouldest bless me indeed, and enlarge my coast, and that thine hand might be with me, and that thou wouldest keep me from evil, that it may not grieve me! And God granted him that which he requested. (1 Chronicles 4:10)*

I pray for you today that the Lord will:

1. Bless you indeed
2. Enlarge your coast
3. Keep His hand upon you
4. Keep you from evil and it will not grieve you
5. Grant your request

KEY POINTS FROM PART FOUR

- Jesus is Our King and is Always Ready to Help.
- We can know that He hears us, all we have to do is ask in accordance with His will which is revealed in His Word.
- It is all about His finished work and has nothing to do with our righteousness.

- With God on our side, who or what can stand against us?
- The Lord is in the business of doing good.
- When you come to God for a solution and He gives you simple instructions, following those instructions always bring divine intervention.
- Our God is still in the business of bringing down walls today.
- There may be areas of your life that are barren, all you need to do is pray and ask the Lord for fruitfulness.
- Promotion comes only from God.

CONCLUSION

GOD'S GREAT AND PRECIOUS PROMISES

Whereby are given unto us exceeding great and precious promises: that by these ye might be partakers of the divine nature, having escaped the corruption that is in the world through lust. (2 Peter 1:4)

For all the promises of God in him are yea, and in him Amen, unto the glory of God by us. (2 Corinthians 1:20)

Let us look in the Bible to see how much God wants to fulfill our desires and meet all our needs when they comply with His word and we come to Him with the right attitude of our heart.

The Lord upholdeth all that fall, and raiseth up all those that be bowed down. The eyes of all wait upon thee; and thou givest them their meat in due season. Thou openest thine hand, and satisfiest the desire of every living thing. The Lord is righteous in all his ways, and holy in all his works. The Lord is nigh unto all them that call upon him, to all that call upon him in truth. He will fulfil the desire of them that fear him: he also will hear their cry, and will save them. (Psalm 145:14-19 emphasis added)

And, behold, a woman, which was diseased with an issue of blood twelve years, came behind him, and touched the hem of his garment: For she said within herself, If I may but touch his garment, I shall be whole. But Jesus turned him about, and when he saw her, he said, Daughter, be of good comfort; thy faith hath made thee whole. And the woman was made whole from that hour. (Matthew 9:20-22 emphasis added)

And it came to pass also on another Sabbath, that he entered into the synagogue and taught: and there was a man whose right hand was withered. And the scribes and Pharisees watched him, whether he would heal on the Sabbath day; that they might find an accusation against him. But he knew their thoughts, and said to the man which had the withered hand, Rise up, and stand forth in the midst. And he arose and stood forth. Then said Jesus unto them, I will ask you one thing; Is it lawful on the Sabbath days to do good, or to do evil? To save life, or to destroy it? And looking round about upon them all, he said unto the man, Stretch forth thy hand. And he did so: and his hand was restored whole as the other. (Luke 6:6-10)

And they came to Jericho: and as he went out of Jericho with his disciples and a great number of people, blind Bartimæus, the son of Timæus, sat by the highway side begging. And when he heard that it was Jesus of Nazareth, he began to cry out, and say, Jesus, thou Son of David, have mercy on me. And many charged him that he should hold his peace: but he cried the more a great deal, Thou Son of David, have mercy on me.

And Jesus stood still, and commanded him to be called. And they call the blind man, saying unto him, Be of good comfort, rise; he calleth thee. And he, casting away his garment, rose, and came to Jesus. And Jesus answered and said unto him, What wilt thou that I should do unto thee? The blind man said unto him, Lord, that I might receive my sight. And Jesus said unto him, Go thy way; thy faith hath made thee whole. And immediately he received his sight, and followed Jesus in the way. (Mark 10:46-52 emphasis added)

God already said yes to all your godly desires in life, so go ahead and enjoy your new life in Christ by accepting His great and precious promises. They are for you so you can be partakers of the divine nature.

Note: Jesus not only heals all our diseases, He also heals spiritual blindness so we can understand all that the scriptures say about God's promises.

And when Jesus was come into Peter's house, he saw his wife's mother laid, and sick of a fever. And he touched her hand, and the fever left her: and she arose, and ministered unto them. (Matthew 8:14-15)

And when he came to his disciples, he saw a great multitude about them, and the scribes questioning with them. And straightway all the people, when they beheld him, were greatly amazed, and running to him saluted him. And one of the multitude answered and said, Master, I have brought unto thee my son, which hath a dumb spirit; When Jesus saw that the people came running together, he rebuked the foul spirit, saying unto him, Thou dumb and deaf spirit, I charge thee, come out of him, and enter no more into him. And the spirit cried, and rent him sore, and came out of him: and he was as one dead;

> *insomuch that many said, He is dead. But Jesus took him by the hand, and lifted him up; and he arose. (Mark 9:14-15, 17, 25-27)*

> *When the even was come, they brought unto him many that were possessed with devils: and he cast out the spirits with his word, and healed all that were sick: That it might be fulfilled which was spoken by Esaias the prophet, saying, Himself took our infirmities, and bare our sicknesses. (Matthew 8:16-17 emphasis added)*

> *And he said unto them, These are the words which I spake unto you, while I was yet with you, that all things must be fulfilled, which were written in the law of Moses, and in the prophets, and in the Psalm, concerning me. Then opened he their understanding, that they might understand the scriptures. (Luke 24:44-45 emphasis added)*

Conclusively, the kingdom of God is righteousness, peace, and joy in the Holy Ghost. Serve God, receive His great and precious promises for you and your family, and enjoy living the kingdom lifestyle!

> *For the kingdom of God is not meat and drink; but righteousness, and peace, and joy in the Holy Ghost. For he that in these things serveth Christ is acceptable to God, and approved of men. (Romans 14:17-18)*

ABOUT THE AUTHOR

Dr. Olalekan Joseph Olowe is a physical therapist by trade and a pastor by calling. Together with his wife, Omolade, they are the Presiding Servants over Kingdom Dominion Ministry International (KDMI) with a ministry base at El Paso, Texas from where they reach out globally.

A graduate of Rocky Mountain University of Health Professionals with a transitional Doctorate in Physical Therapy, Joseph is blessed with a physical therapy practice in El Paso, Texas.

He's a prolific writer and the author of I Am Three Dimensional, Living Free: The Power of Self-Control amongst other books. He's happily married to Omolade and they are blessed with three children.

KINGDOM DOMINION MINISTRY INTERNATIONAL (KDMI)

To partner with us or to be part of Kingdom Dominion Ministry International (KDMI), please call or write us

1 800-561-9170 or + 1 915-478-8807

P. O Box 10499
El Paso, TX 79995

info@hisdominion.org | www.hisdominion.org